Concentration Camps: A Very Short Introduction

Praise for the hardback, *Concentration Camps*

'This concise book provides a wealth of insights, and suggestive, but plausible, arguments on the origins, myriad functions, and mutability of the most horrifying institution of the twentieth century. It is full of clear thinking and tough talking, which is necessary, since the subject makes most of us recoil in horror and retreat into comfortable moral judgments about the singularity of the Nazi crimes.'

Alan Kramer, Trinity College Dublin

Very Short Introductions available now:

ABOLITIONISM Richard S. Newman
ACCOUNTING Christopher Nobes
ADAM SMITH Christopher J. Berry
ADOLESCENCE Peter K. Smith
ADVERTISING Winston Fletcher
AFRICAN AMERICAN RELIGION
    Eddie S. Glaude Jr
AFRICAN HISTORY John Parker and
    Richard Rathbone
AFRICAN POLITICS Ian Taylor
AFRICAN RELIGIONS
    Jacob K. Olupona
AGEING Nancy A. Pachana
AGNOSTICISM Robin Le Poidevin
AGRICULTURE Paul Brassley and
    Richard Soffe
ALEXANDER THE GREAT
    Hugh Bowden
ALGEBRA Peter M. Higgins
AMERICAN CULTURAL HISTORY
    Eric Avila
AMERICAN HISTORY Paul S. Boyer
AMERICAN IMMIGRATION
    David A. Gerber
AMERICAN LEGAL HISTORY
    G. Edward White
AMERICAN NAVAL HISTORY
    Craig L. Symonds
AMERICAN POLITICAL HISTORY
    Donald Critchlow
AMERICAN POLITICAL PARTIES
    AND ELECTIONS L. Sandy Maisel
AMERICAN POLITICS
    Richard M. Valelly
THE AMERICAN PRESIDENCY
    Charles O. Jones
THE AMERICAN REVOLUTION
    Robert J. Allison
AMERICAN SLAVERY
    Heather Andrea Williams
THE AMERICAN WEST Stephen Aron
AMERICAN WOMEN'S HISTORY
    Susan Ware
ANAESTHESIA Aidan O'Donnell
ANALYTIC PHILOSOPHY
    Michael Beaney
ANARCHISM Colin Ward
ANCIENT ASSYRIA Karen Radner
ANCIENT EGYPT Ian Shaw
ANCIENT EGYPTIAN ART AND
    ARCHITECTURE Christina Riggs
ANCIENT GREECE Paul Cartledge
THE ANCIENT NEAR EAST
    Amanda H. Podany
ANCIENT PHILOSOPHY Julia Annas
ANCIENT WARFARE
    Harry Sidebottom
ANGELS David Albert Jones
ANGLICANISM Mark Chapman
THE ANGLO-SAXON AGE John Blair
ANIMAL BEHAVIOUR
    Tristram D. Wyatt
THE ANIMAL KINGDOM
    Peter Holland
ANIMAL RIGHTS David DeGrazia
THE ANTARCTIC Klaus Dodds
ANTHROPOCENE Erle C. Ellis
ANTISEMITISM Steven Beller

ANXIETY Daniel Freeman and
Jason Freeman
APPLIED MATHEMATICS
Alain Goriely
THE APOCRYPHAL GOSPELS
Paul Foster
ARCHAEOLOGY Paul Bahn
ARCHITECTURE Andrew Ballantyne
ARISTOCRACY William Doyle
ARISTOTLE Jonathan Barnes
ART HISTORY Dana Arnold
ART THEORY Cynthia Freeland
ARTIFICIAL INTELLIGENCE
Margaret A. Boden
ASIAN AMERICAN HISTORY
Madeline Y. Hsu
ASTROBIOLOGY David C. Catling
ASTROPHYSICS James Binney
ATHEISM Julian Baggini
THE ATMOSPHERE Paul I. Palmer
AUGUSTINE Henry Chadwick
AUSTRALIA Kenneth Morgan
AUTISM Uta Frith
AUTOBIOGRAPHY Laura Marcus
THE AVANT GARDE David Cottington
THE AZTECS David Carrasco
BABYLONIA Trevor Bryce
BACTERIA Sebastian G. B. Amyes
BANKING John Goddard and
John O. S. Wilson
BARTHES Jonathan Culler
THE BEATS David Sterritt
BEAUTY Roger Scruton
BEHAVIOURAL ECONOMICS
Michelle Baddeley
BESTSELLERS John Sutherland
THE BIBLE John Riches
BIBLICAL ARCHAEOLOGY
Eric H. Cline
BIG DATA Dawn E. Holmes
BIOGRAPHY Hermione Lee
BIOMETRICS Michael Fairhurst
BLACK HOLES Katherine Blundell
BLOOD Chris Cooper
THE BLUES Elijah Wald
THE BODY Chris Shilling
THE BOOK OF COMMON PRAYER
Brian Cummings
THE BOOK OF MORMON
Terryl Givens

BORDERS Alexander C. Diener and
Joshua Hagen
THE BRAIN Michael O'Shea
BRANDING Robert Jones
THE BRICS Andrew F. Cooper
THE BRITISH CONSTITUTION
Martin Loughlin
THE BRITISH EMPIRE Ashley Jackson
BRITISH POLITICS Anthony Wright
BUDDHA Michael Carrithers
BUDDHISM Damien Keown
BUDDHIST ETHICS Damien Keown
BYZANTIUM Peter Sarris
C. S. LEWIS James Como
CALVINISM Jon Balserak
CANCER Nicholas James
CAPITALISM James Fulcher
CATHOLICISM Gerald O'Collins
CAUSATION Stephen Mumford
and Rani Lill Anjum
THE CELL Terence Allen and
Graham Cowling
THE CELTS Barry Cunliffe
CHAOS Leonard Smith
CHARLES DICKENS Jenny Hartley
CHEMISTRY Peter Atkins
CHILD PSYCHOLOGY Usha Goswami
CHILDREN'S LITERATURE
Kimberley Reynolds
CHINESE LITERATURE Sabina Knight
CHOICE THEORY Michael Allingham
CHRISTIAN ART Beth Williamson
CHRISTIAN ETHICS D. Stephen Long
CHRISTIANITY Linda Woodhead
CIRCADIAN RHYTHMS
Russell Foster and Leon Kreitzman
CITIZENSHIP Richard Bellamy
CIVIL ENGINEERING
David Muir Wood
CLASSICAL LITERATURE William Allan
CLASSICAL MYTHOLOGY
Helen Morales
CLASSICS Mary Beard and
John Henderson
CLAUSEWITZ Michael Howard
CLIMATE Mark Maslin
CLIMATE CHANGE Mark Maslin
CLINICAL PSYCHOLOGY
Susan Llewelyn and
Katie Aafjes-van Doorn

COGNITIVE NEUROSCIENCE
   Richard Passingham
THE COLD WAR Robert McMahon
COLONIAL AMERICA Alan Taylor
COLONIAL LATIN AMERICAN
   LITERATURE Rolena Adorno
COMBINATORICS Robin Wilson
COMEDY Matthew Bevis
COMMUNISM Leslie Holmes
COMPARATIVE LITERATURE
   Ben Hutchinson
COMPLEXITY John H. Holland
THE COMPUTER Darrel Ince
COMPUTER SCIENCE
   Subrata Dasgupta
CONCENTRATION CAMPS
   Dan Stone
CONFUCIANISM Daniel K. Gardner
THE CONQUISTADORS
   Matthew Restall and
   Felipe Fernández-Armesto
CONSCIENCE Paul Strohm
CONSCIOUSNESS Susan Blackmore
CONTEMPORARY ART
   Julian Stallabrass
CONTEMPORARY FICTION
   Robert Eaglestone
CONTINENTAL PHILOSOPHY
   Simon Critchley
COPERNICUS Owen Gingerich
CORAL REEFS Charles Sheppard
CORPORATE SOCIAL
   RESPONSIBILITY Jeremy Moon
CORRUPTION Leslie Holmes
COSMOLOGY Peter Coles
CRIME FICTION Richard Bradford
CRIMINAL JUSTICE Julian V. Roberts
CRIMINOLOGY Tim Newburn
CRITICAL THEORY
   Stephen Eric Bronner
THE CRUSADES Christopher Tyerman
CRYPTOGRAPHY Fred Piper and
   Sean Murphy
CRYSTALLOGRAPHY A. M. Glazer
THE CULTURAL REVOLUTION
   Richard Curt Kraus
DADA AND SURREALISM
   David Hopkins
DANTE Peter Hainsworth and
   David Robey

DARWIN Jonathan Howard
THE DEAD SEA SCROLLS
   Timothy H. Lim
DECADENCE David Weir
DECOLONIZATION Dane Kennedy
DEMOCRACY Bernard Crick
DEMOGRAPHY Sarah Harper
DEPRESSION Jan Scott and
   Mary Jane Tacchi
DERRIDA Simon Glendinning
DESCARTES Tom Sorell
DESERTS Nick Middleton
DESIGN John Heskett
DEVELOPMENT Ian Goldin
DEVELOPMENTAL BIOLOGY
   Lewis Wolpert
THE DEVIL Darren Oldridge
DIASPORA Kevin Kenny
DICTIONARIES Lynda Mugglestone
DINOSAURS David Norman
DIPLOMACY Joseph M. Siracusa
DOCUMENTARY FILM
   Patricia Aufderheide
DREAMING J. Allan Hobson
DRUGS Les Iversen
DRUIDS Barry Cunliffe
EARLY MUSIC Thomas Forrest Kelly
THE EARTH Martin Redfern
EARTH SYSTEM SCIENCE Tim Lenton
ECONOMICS Partha Dasgupta
EDUCATION Gary Thomas
EGYPTIAN MYTH Geraldine Pinch
EIGHTEENTH-CENTURY BRITAIN
   Paul Langford
THE ELEMENTS Philip Ball
EMOTION Dylan Evans
EMPIRE Stephen Howe
ENGELS Terrell Carver
ENGINEERING David Blockley
THE ENGLISH LANGUAGE
   Simon Horobin
ENGLISH LITERATURE Jonathan Bate
THE ENLIGHTENMENT
   John Robertson
ENTREPRENEURSHIP
   Paul Westhead and Mike Wright
ENVIRONMENTAL ECONOMICS
   Stephen Smith
ENVIRONMENTAL ETHICS
   Robin Attfield

ENVIRONMENTAL LAW
   Elizabeth Fisher
ENVIRONMENTAL POLITICS
   Andrew Dobson
EPICUREANISM Catherine Wilson
EPIDEMIOLOGY Rodolfo Saracci
ETHICS Simon Blackburn
ETHNOMUSICOLOGY Timothy Rice
THE ETRUSCANS Christopher Smith
EUGENICS Philippa Levine
THE EUROPEAN UNION
   Simon Usherwood and John Pinder
EUROPEAN UNION LAW
   Anthony Arnull
EVOLUTION Brian and
   Deborah Charlesworth
EXISTENTIALISM Thomas Flynn
EXPLORATION Stewart A. Weaver
THE EYE Michael Land
FAIRY TALE Marina Warner
FAMILY LAW Jonathan Herring
FASCISM Kevin Passmore
FASHION Rebecca Arnold
FEMINISM Margaret Walters
FILM Michael Wood
FILM MUSIC Kathryn Kalinak
THE FIRST WORLD WAR
   Michael Howard
FOLK MUSIC Mark Slobin
FILM NOIR James Naremore
FOOD John Krebs
FORENSIC PSYCHOLOGY
   David Canter
FORENSIC SCIENCE Jim Fraser
FORESTS Jaboury Ghazoul
FOSSILS Keith Thomson
FOUCAULT Gary Gutting
THE FOUNDING FATHERS
   R. B. Bernstein
FRACTALS Kenneth Falconer
FREE SPEECH Nigel Warburton
FREE WILL Thomas Pink
FREEMASONRY Andreas Önnerfors
FRENCH LITERATURE John D. Lyons
THE FRENCH REVOLUTION
   William Doyle
FREUD Anthony Storr
FUNDAMENTALISM Malise Ruthven
FUNGI Nicholas P. Money
THE FUTURE Jennifer M. Gidley

GALAXIES John Gribbin
GALILEO Stillman Drake
GAME THEORY Ken Binmore
GANDHI Bhikhu Parekh
GARDEN HISTORY Gordon Campbell
GENES Jonathan Slack
GENIUS Andrew Robinson
GENOMICS John Archibald
GEOGRAPHY John Matthews
   and David Herbert
GEOLOGY Jan Zalasiewicz
GEOPHYSICS William Lowrie
GEOPOLITICS Klaus Dodds
GERMAN LITERATURE Nicholas Boyle
GERMAN PHILOSOPHY
   Andrew Bowie
GLACIATION David J. A. Evans
GLOBAL CATASTROPHES Bill McGuire
GLOBAL ECONOMIC HISTORY
   Robert C. Allen
GLOBALIZATION Manfred Steger
GOD John Bowker
GOETHE Ritchie Robertson
THE GOTHIC Nick Groom
GOVERNANCE Mark Bevir
GRAVITY Timothy Clifton
THE GREAT DEPRESSION AND
   THE NEW DEAL Eric Rauchway
HABERMAS James Gordon Finlayson
THE HABSBURG EMPIRE
   Martyn Rady
HAPPINESS Daniel M. Haybron
THE HARLEM RENAISSANCE
   Cheryl A. Wall
THE HEBREW BIBLE AS LITERATURE
   Tod Linafelt
HEGEL Peter Singer
HEIDEGGER Michael Inwood
THE HELLENISTIC AGE
   Peter Thonemann
HEREDITY John Waller
HERMENEUTICS Jens Zimmermann
HERODOTUS Jennifer T. Roberts
HIEROGLYPHS Penelope Wilson
HINDUISM Kim Knott
HISTORY John H. Arnold
THE HISTORY OF ASTRONOMY
   Michael Hoskin
THE HISTORY OF CHEMISTRY
   William H. Brock

THE HISTORY OF CHILDHOOD
James Marten
THE HISTORY OF CINEMA
Geoffrey Nowell-Smith
THE HISTORY OF LIFE
Michael Benton
THE HISTORY OF MATHEMATICS
Jacqueline Stedall
THE HISTORY OF MEDICINE
William Bynum
THE HISTORY OF PHYSICS
J. L. Heilbron
THE HISTORY OF TIME
Leofranc Holford-Strevens
HIV AND AIDS Alan Whiteside
HOBBES Richard Tuck
HOLLYWOOD Peter Decherney
THE HOLY ROMAN EMPIRE
Joachim Whaley
HOME Michael Allen Fox
HOMER Barbara Graziosi
HORMONES Martin Luck
HUMAN ANATOMY Leslie Klenerman
HUMAN EVOLUTION Bernard Wood
HUMAN RIGHTS Andrew Clapham
HUMANISM Stephen Law
HUME A. J. Ayer
HUMOUR Noël Carroll
THE ICE AGE Jamie Woodward
IDENTITY Florian Coulmas
IDEOLOGY Michael Freeden
THE IMMUNE SYSTEM
Paul Klenerman
INDIAN CINEMA Ashish Rajadhyaksha
INDIAN PHILOSOPHY Sue Hamilton
THE INDUSTRIAL REVOLUTION
Robert C. Allen
INFECTIOUS DISEASE Marta L. Wayne
and Benjamin M. Bolker
INFINITY Ian Stewart
INFORMATION Luciano Floridi
INNOVATION Mark Dodgson
and David Gann
INTELLIGENCE Ian J. Deary
INTELLECTUAL PROPERTY
Siva Vaidhyanathan
INTERNATIONAL LAW
Vaughan Lowe
INTERNATIONAL MIGRATION
Khalid Koser

INTERNATIONAL RELATIONS
Paul Wilkinson
INTERNATIONAL SECURITY
Christopher S. Browning
IRAN Ali M. Ansari
ISLAM Malise Ruthven
ISLAMIC HISTORY Adam Silverstein
ISOTOPES Rob Ellam
ITALIAN LITERATURE
Peter Hainsworth and David Robey
JESUS Richard Bauckham
JEWISH HISTORY David N. Myers
JOURNALISM Ian Hargreaves
JUDAISM Norman Solomon
JUNG Anthony Stevens
KABBALAH Joseph Dan
KAFKA Ritchie Robertson
KANT Roger Scruton
KEYNES Robert Skidelsky
KIERKEGAARD Patrick Gardiner
KNOWLEDGE Jennifer Nagel
THE KORAN Michael Cook
LAKES Warwick F. Vincent
LANDSCAPE ARCHITECTURE
Ian H. Thompson
LANDSCAPES AND
GEOMORPHOLOGY
Andrew Goudie and Heather Viles
LANGUAGES Stephen R. Anderson
LATE ANTIQUITY Gillian Clark
LAW Raymond Wacks
THE LAWS OF THERMODYNAMICS
Peter Atkins
LEADERSHIP Keith Grint
LEARNING Mark Haselgrove
LEIBNIZ Maria Rosa Antognazza
LIBERALISM Michael Freeden
LIGHT Ian Walmsley
LINCOLN Allen C. Guelzo
LINGUISTICS Peter Matthews
LITERARY THEORY Jonathan Culler
LOCKE John Dunn
LOGIC Graham Priest
LOVE Ronald de Sousa
MACHIAVELLI Quentin Skinner
MADNESS Andrew Scull
MAGIC Owen Davies
MAGNA CARTA Nicholas Vincent
MAGNETISM Stephen Blundell
MALTHUS Donald Winch

MAMMALS T. S. Kemp
MANAGEMENT John Hendry
MAO Delia Davin
MARINE BIOLOGY Philip V. Mladenov
THE MARQUIS DE SADE John Phillips
MARTIN LUTHER Scott H. Hendrix
MARTYRDOM Jolyon Mitchell
MARX Peter Singer
MATERIALS Christopher Hall
MATHEMATICS Timothy Gowers
MATHEMATICAL FINANCE
    Mark H. A. Davis
MATTER Geoff Cottrell
THE MEANING OF LIFE
    Terry Eagleton
MEASUREMENT David Hand
MEDICAL ETHICS Michael Dunn
    and Tony Hope
MEDICAL LAW Charles Foster
MEDIEVAL BRITAIN John Gillingham
    and Ralph A. Griffiths
MEDIEVAL LITERATURE
    Elaine Treharne
MEDIEVAL PHILOSOPHY
    John Marenbon
MEMORY Jonathan K. Foster
METAPHYSICS Stephen Mumford
THE MEXICAN REVOLUTION
    Alan Knight
MICHAEL FARADAY
    Frank A. J. L. James
MICROBIOLOGY Nicholas P. Money
MICROECONOMICS Avinash Dixit
MICROSCOPY Terence Allen
THE MIDDLE AGES Miri Rubin
MILITARY JUSTICE Eugene R. Fidell
MILITARY STRATEGY
    Antulio J. Echevarria II
MINERALS David Vaughan
MIRACLES Yujin Nagasawa
MODERN ARCHITECTURE
    Adam Sharr
MODERN ART David Cottington
MODERN CHINA Rana Mitter
MODERN DRAMA
    Kirsten E. Shepherd-Barr
MODERN FRANCE
    Vanessa R. Schwartz
MODERN INDIA Craig Jeffrey
MODERN IRELAND Senia Pašeta

MODERN ITALY Anna Cento Bull
MODERN JAPAN
    Christopher Goto-Jones
MODERN LATIN AMERICAN
    LITERATURE
    Roberto González Echevarría
MODERN WAR Richard English
MODERNISM Christopher Butler
MOLECULAR BIOLOGY
    Aysha Divan and Janice A. Royds
MOLECULES Philip Ball
MONASTICISM Stephen J. Davis
THE MONGOLS Morris Rossabi
MOONS David A. Rothery
MORMONISM
    Richard Lyman Bushman
MOUNTAINS Martin F. Price
MUHAMMAD Jonathan A. C. Brown
MULTICULTURALISM Ali Rattansi
MULTILINGUALISM John C. Maher
MUSIC Nicholas Cook
MYTH Robert A. Segal
NAPOLEON David Bell
THE NAPOLEONIC WARS
    Mike Rapport
NATIONALISM Steven Grosby
NATIVE AMERICAN LITERATURE
    Sean Teuton
NAVIGATION Jim Bennett
NELSON MANDELA Elleke Boehmer
NEOLIBERALISM Manfred Steger
    and Ravi Roy
NETWORKS Guido Caldarelli and
    Michele Catanzaro
THE NEW TESTAMENT
    Luke Timothy Johnson
THE NEW TESTAMENT AS
    LITERATURE Kyle Keefer
NEWTON Robert Iliffe
NIETZSCHE Michael Tanner
NINETEENTH-CENTURY BRITAIN
    Christopher Harvie and
    H. C. G. Matthew
THE NORMAN CONQUEST
    George Garnett
NORTH AMERICAN INDIANS
    Theda Perdue and Michael D. Green
NORTHERN IRELAND
    Marc Mulholland
NOTHING Frank Close

NUCLEAR PHYSICS Frank Close
NUCLEAR POWER Maxwell Irvine
NUCLEAR WEAPONS
    Joseph M. Siracusa
NUMBERS Peter M. Higgins
NUTRITION David A. Bender
OBJECTIVITY Stephen Gaukroger
OCEANS Dorrik Stow
THE OLD TESTAMENT
    Michael D. Coogan
THE ORCHESTRA D. Kern Holoman
ORGANIC CHEMISTRY
    Graham Patrick
ORGANIZED CRIME
    Georgios A. Antonopoulos and
    Georgios Papanicolaou
ORGANIZATIONS Mary Jo Hatch
PAGANISM Owen Davies
PAIN Rob Boddice
THE PALESTINIAN-ISRAELI
    CONFLICT Martin Bunton
PANDEMICS Christian W. McMillen
PARTICLE PHYSICS Frank Close
PAUL E. P. Sanders
PEACE Oliver P. Richmond
PENTECOSTALISM William K. Kay
PERCEPTION Brian Rogers
THE PERIODIC TABLE Eric R. Scerri
PHILOSOPHY Edward Craig
PHILOSOPHY IN THE ISLAMIC
    WORLD Peter Adamson
PHILOSOPHY OF LAW
    Raymond Wacks
PHILOSOPHY OF SCIENCE
    Samir Okasha
PHILOSOPHY OF RELIGION
    Tim Bayne
PHOTOGRAPHY Steve Edwards
PHYSICAL CHEMISTRY Peter Atkins
PILGRIMAGE Ian Reader
PLAGUE Paul Slack
PLANETS David A. Rothery
PLANTS Timothy Walker
PLATE TECTONICS Peter Molnar
PLATO Julia Annas
POLITICAL PHILOSOPHY
    David Miller
POLITICS Kenneth Minogue
POPULISM Cas Mudde and
    Cristóbal Rovira Kaltwasser

POSTCOLONIALISM Robert Young
POSTMODERNISM Christopher Butler
POSTSTRUCTURALISM
    Catherine Belsey
POVERTY Philip N. Jefferson
PREHISTORY Chris Gosden
PRESOCRATIC PHILOSOPHY
    Catherine Osborne
PRIVACY Raymond Wacks
PROBABILITY John Haigh
PROGRESSIVISM Walter Nugent
PROJECTS Andrew Davies
PROTESTANTISM Mark A. Noll
PSYCHIATRY Tom Burns
PSYCHOANALYSIS Daniel Pick
PSYCHOLOGY Gillian Butler and
    Freda McManus
PSYCHOLOGY OF MUSIC
    Elizabeth Hellmuth Margulis
PSYCHOTHERAPY Tom Burns and
    Eva Burns-Lundgren
PUBLIC ADMINISTRATION
    Stella Z. Theodoulou and Ravi K. Roy
PUBLIC HEALTH Virginia Berridge
PURITANISM Francis J. Bremer
THE QUAKERS Pink Dandelion
QUANTUM THEORY
    John Polkinghorne
RACISM Ali Rattansi
RADIOACTIVITY Claudio Tuniz
RASTAFARI Ennis B. Edmonds
THE REAGAN REVOLUTION Gil Troy
REALITY Jan Westerhoff
THE REFORMATION Peter Marshall
RELATIVITY Russell Stannard
RELIGION IN AMERICA Timothy Beal
THE RENAISSANCE Jerry Brotton
RENAISSANCE ART
    Geraldine A. Johnson
REPTILES T. S. Kemp
REVOLUTIONS Jack A. Goldstone
RHETORIC Richard Toye
RISK Baruch Fischhoff and John Kadvany
RITUAL Barry Stephenson
RIVERS Nick Middleton
ROBOTICS Alan Winfield
ROCKS Jan Zalasiewicz
ROMAN BRITAIN Peter Salway
THE ROMAN EMPIRE
    Christopher Kelly

THE ROMAN REPUBLIC
David M. Gwynn
ROMANTICISM Michael Ferber
ROUSSEAU Robert Wokler
RUSSELL A. C. Grayling
RUSSIAN HISTORY Geoffrey Hosking
RUSSIAN LITERATURE Catriona Kelly
THE RUSSIAN REVOLUTION
S. A. Smith
THE SAINTS Simon Yarrow
SAVANNAS Peter A. Furley
SCHIZOPHRENIA Chris Frith and
Eve Johnstone
SCHOPENHAUER
Christopher Janaway
SCIENCE AND RELIGION
Thomas Dixon
SCIENCE FICTION David Seed
THE SCIENTIFIC REVOLUTION
Lawrence M. Principe
SCOTLAND Rab Houston
SEXUAL SELECTION Marlene Zuk
and Leigh W. Simmons
SEXUALITY Véronique Mottier
SHAKESPEARE'S COMEDIES
Bart van Es
SHAKESPEARE'S SONNETS AND
POEMS Jonathan F. S. Post
SHAKESPEARE'S TRAGEDIES
Stanley Wells
SIKHISM Eleanor Nesbitt
THE SILK ROAD James A. Millward
SLANG Jonathon Green
SLEEP Steven W. Lockley and
Russell G. Foster
SOCIAL AND CULTURAL
ANTHROPOLOGY
John Monaghan and Peter Just
SOCIAL PSYCHOLOGY Richard J. Crisp
SOCIAL WORK Sally Holland
and Jonathan Scourfield
SOCIALISM Michael Newman
SOCIOLINGUISTICS John Edwards
SOCIOLOGY Steve Bruce
SOCRATES C. C. W. Taylor
SOUND Mike Goldsmith
SOUTHEAST ASIA James R. Rush
THE SOVIET UNION Stephen Lovell
THE SPANISH CIVIL WAR
Helen Graham

SPANISH LITERATURE Jo Labanyi
SPINOZA Roger Scruton
SPIRITUALITY Philip Sheldrake
SPORT Mike Cronin
STARS Andrew King
STATISTICS David J. Hand
STEM CELLS Jonathan Slack
STOICISM Brad Inwood
STRUCTURAL ENGINEERING
David Blockley
STUART BRITAIN John Morrill
SUPERCONDUCTIVITY
Stephen Blundell
SYMMETRY Ian Stewart
SYNTHETIC BIOLOGY Jamie A. Davies
TAXATION Stephen Smith
TEETH Peter S. Ungar
TELESCOPES Geoff Cottrell
TERRORISM Charles Townshend
THEATRE Marvin Carlson
THEOLOGY David F. Ford
THINKING AND REASONING
Jonathan St B. T. Evans
THOMAS AQUINAS Fergus Kerr
THOUGHT Tim Bayne
TIBETAN BUDDHISM
Matthew T. Kapstein
TOCQUEVILLE Harvey C. Mansfield
TRAGEDY Adrian Poole
TRANSLATION Matthew Reynolds
THE TREATY OF VERSAILLES
Michael S. Neiberg
THE TROJAN WAR Eric H. Cline
TRUST Katherine Hawley
THE TUDORS John Guy
TWENTIETH-CENTURY BRITAIN
Kenneth O. Morgan
TYPOGRAPHY Paul Luna
THE UNITED NATIONS
Jussi M. Hanhimäki
UNIVERSITIES AND COLLEGES
David Palfreyman and Paul Temple
THE U.S. CONGRESS Donald A. Ritchie
THE U.S. CONSTITUTION
David J. Bodenhamer
THE U.S. SUPREME COURT
Linda Greenhouse
UTILITARIANISM
Katarzyna de Lazari-Radek and
Peter Singer

UTOPIANISM Lyman Tower Sargent
VETERINARY SCIENCE James Yeates
THE VIKINGS Julian D. Richards
VIRUSES Dorothy H. Crawford
VOLTAIRE Nicholas Cronk
WAR AND TECHNOLOGY
    Alex Roland
WATER John Finney
WAVES Mike Goldsmith
WEATHER Storm Dunlop
THE WELFARE STATE David Garland

WILLIAM SHAKESPEARE Stanley Wells
WITCHCRAFT Malcolm Gaskill
WITTGENSTEIN A. C. Grayling
WORK Stephen Fineman
WORLD MUSIC Philip Bohlman
THE WORLD TRADE
    ORGANIZATION Amrita Narlikar
WORLD WAR II Gerhard L. Weinberg
WRITING AND SCRIPT
    Andrew Robinson
ZIONISM Michael Stanislawski

Available soon:

METHODISM William J. Abraham
TOLSTOY Liza Knapp
SYNAESTHESIA Julia Simner

READING Belinda Jack
THE TREATY OF VERSAILLES
    Michael S. Neiberg

For more information visit our website

www.oup.com/vsi/

Dan Stone

CONCENTRATION CAMPS

A Very Short Introduction

OXFORD
UNIVERSITY PRESS

OXFORD

UNIVERSITY PRESS

Great Clarendon Street, Oxford, OX2 6DP,
United Kingdom

Oxford University Press is a department of the University of Oxford.
It furthers the University's objective of excellence in research, scholarship,
and education by publishing worldwide. Oxford is a registered trade mark of
Oxford University Press in the UK and in certain other countries

© Dan Stone 2019

The moral rights of the author have been asserted

First published in hardback as *Concentration Camps* 2017
First published as a *Very Short Introduction* 2019

Impression: 1

Published in the United States of America by Oxford University Press
198 Madison Avenue, New York, NY 10016, United States of America

British Library Cataloguing in Publication Data
Data available

Library of Congress Control Number: 2018962714

ISBN 978-0-19-872338-7

Printed in Great Britain by
Ashford Colour Press Ltd, Gosport, Hampshire

Links to third party websites are provided by Oxford in good faith and
for information only. Oxford disclaims any responsibility for the materials
contained in any third party website referenced in this work.

Contents

Preface and acknowledgements xv

List of illustrations xvii

1 What is a concentration camp? 1

2 Origins 10

3 The Third Reich's world of camps 30

4 The Gulag 50

5 The wide world of camps 69

6 'An Auschwitz every three months': society as camp? 94

References 115

Further reading 127

Publisher's acknowledgements 131

Index 133

Preface and acknowledgements

A book such as this must aim not to be comprehensive but to ask relevant questions. This book ranges widely, drawing on a voluminous scholarly literature, and I hope that readers will find some clearly defended opinions and some suggestions for thinking about the topic in greater detail. But most of all I hope that they will not expect all the answers; if the questions I raise are thought-provoking then the book has done its job. There are many other paths to follow than those taken here and I hope the book will encourage readers to go down some of them. This is an unpleasant topic but one that can hardly be sidestepped if one is interested in the nature of the modern world. I have not spent too much time on highfalutin theories of what it all means—though I linger with some of these ideas in the final chapter—because I wanted to explore the ways in which different sorts of concentration camps have emerged in different political, social, geographical, and chronological contexts over the last century or so. Only by knowing something of the history of concentration camps can one begin to consider their meaning for our civilization. The book is therefore arranged more or less chronologically, only turning at the end to address theories of what concentration camps tell us about the modern world.

Many friends and colleagues have helped me along the way. Not least of these are the many scholars on whose work I have drawn, details of which can be found in the references and suggestions for further reading. Some of the ideas in this book were tested at seminars at the University of Michigan, Ann Arbor, the University of Bucharest, the University of Sussex, and the University of Southern California, and I'm grateful to colleagues at those institutions for their input. I am especially grateful to my colleagues who put me right on numerous points of fact, who have challenged me to set my ideas out more clearly, or otherwise helped shape the book. In particular, it's a pleasure to record my thanks to Daniel Beer, Anne Berg, Mark Donnelly, Geoff Eley, Christian Goeschel, Michelle Gordon, Helen Graham, Wolf Gruner, Becky Jinks, Christoph Kreutzmüller, Florin Lobonţ, Robert Priest, and Nikolaus Wachsmann for providing me with useful references and for taking the time to read some or all of the book in draft form. I would especially like to thank Jens Meierhenrich, who provided a very careful and helpful reading of the manuscript.

List of illustrations

1 Norvals Pont camp in
South Africa during the
Anglo-Boer War **15**
© TopFoto.

2 Shark Island, German
South-West Africa
(Namibia) **18**
© Ullsteinbild/TopFoto.

3 Inmates performing slave
labour, 28 July 1938 **33**
Bundesarchiv, Bild 152-23-10A/
Photo: Friedrich Franz Bauer.

4 Map of the Gulags in
the USSR **52**

5 Vorkuta industrial
concentration camp complex,
160 km above the Arctic Circle,
with Gulag camp of coal mine
nos 9–10 in the foreground
and coal mine 'Kapitlanya'
on the horizon, 1955 **56**
Gulag Collection/Tomasz Kizny.

6 'What about Us, Mr
Macmillan?', David Low
cartoon, *Evening Standard*,
26 February 1943 **74**
Solo Syndication. Photo: British
Cartoon Archive.

7 'Waiting for the Signal from
Home', Dr Seuss cartoon,
PM, 13 February 1942 **77**
The Granger Collection/TopFoto.

8 One of the Mau Mau
camps **86**
Stroud/Stringer/Getty Images.

9 'Freedom Thru Detention',
Dave Brown cartoon,
Independent, 19 April
2000 **95**
Photo: British Cartoon Archive.

10 Ruins at Christianstadt **111**
© Jan Faktor.

Chapter 1
What is a concentration camp?

In his summing up at the trial of Oswald Pohl et al., one of the
so-called 'subsequent trials' at Nuremberg, Judge Michael
Musmanno noted that:

> In the general lurid picture of World War II, with its wrecked cities,
> uprooted farmland, demolished transportation facilities, and public
> utilities, starvation, disease, ashes, death, rubble, and dust, one item
> of horror seems to stand out with particularly dramatic and tragic
> intensity—the concentration camp. It can be seriously doubted in
> the world of today, even among the most meagerly informed
> peoples that there exists a man or woman who in some manner or
> other has not heard of and recoiled at the mention of the phrase
> concentration camp.

> (NMT, Vol. 5, 1067)

If this were true in 1946, how more true it must be today. The
Holocaust has become in much of the world the ultimate signifier
of evil; at its heart lay the Nazi concentration and death camps.
Since then the world has not only learnt more about the Nazi
camps but has discovered that concentration camps originated
several decades before the Third Reich began using them, and
has witnessed their use again in numerous locations, from wars
of decolonization in Africa to the Yugoslav Wars of the 1990s.
No wonder that Zygmunt Bauman calls the 20th century

'the century of camps'; they have become defining symbols of humankind's lowest point and basest acts. Indeed, for some thinkers, concentration camps are nothing less than the key to understanding modernity, 'the *nomos* of the modern' as philosopher Giorgio Agamben puts it.

This short book will address these grand claims but it will begin on a more prosaic basis, because before we can pronounce on the significance of concentration camps for the modern world we need to be clear about what they are and how they have developed. We need a history of the concentration camp in order to consider why this institution is so important to modern consciousness and identity. First, the book will trace the concentration camp's origins in 19th-century colonial settings such as Australia and the United States, in Cuba, South Africa, and German South-West Africa (today Namibia) in the last years of the 19th and first years of the 20th centuries, and in the genocide of the Armenians during the last days of the Ottoman Empire. It will go on to examine the Nazi camp system, comparing labour camps devised to build the 'racial community' with concentration camps set up to exclude and eventually to eradicate unwanted others. It will show that the images and testimonies of the liberation of the Nazi camps have shaped our definition of concentration camps. It will then go on to examine the Stalinist system of camps and 'special settlements' known as the Gulag and compare the totalitarian countries' use of camps with those of other, less well-known settings, such as the American internment of Japanese-American citizens during the Second World War, Franco's camps during and after the Spanish Civil War, Britain's use of camps for Jewish displaced persons (DPs) in Cyprus trying to reach Palestine after the Second World War, the colonial powers' resort to camps during the wars of decolonization, such as in Algeria, Malaya, and Kenya, the Chinese use of camps during the Maoist period, the Khmer Rouge's attempt to turn the whole of Cambodia into a giant concentration camp in the 1970s, the reappearance of concentration camps during the genocide in Bosnia in the 1990s, and the contemporary camp system in North Korea. I will show that this widespread use of concentration camps is not a coincidence; it tells us something about the modern state and about the ways in which such practices were learned, borrowed, and spread from one place to another.

Lastly, the book will examine the meaning and significance of the concentration camp. Are concentration camps 'states of exception' divorced from society and the rule of law, and, if so, do they therefore function as windows onto the deeper desires of modern states' leaders, or are they aberrant sites? Can a meaningful comparison be made between concentration camps such as the Nazis' and refugee camps or detention centres? What about contemporary settings such as favelas, shanty towns, and sweatshops in the global south? That such questions can be posed suggests that sociologists and philosophers who have asked them are not troubled only by the historical existence of concentration camps but by the possibility that for large sections of today's population the world is effectively a giant concentration camp. There is clearly a need to obtain clarity over the concentration camp's history so that distinctions can be drawn between meaningful insight and political polemic. I will suggest that although concentration camps exist on a continuum of carceral practices that includes prisons, detention centres, and extraterritorial holding pens such as Guantánamo Bay, and although there is no easy or one-size-fits-all definition to be found, yet there is something that distinguishes concentration camps from other sorts of camps where civilians are temporarily held against their will, such as DP camps, internally displaced persons (IDP) camps, or refugee camps. This book will offer an up-to-date history of concentration camps in a global setting and engage with the philosophical literature dealing with the complex question of what the camps tell us about the nature of the modern world.

What is a concentration camp? A working definition is that it is *an isolated, circumscribed site with fixed structures designed to incarcerate civilians.* A concentration camp is not normally a death camp, although death camps in the context of the Holocaust obviously derived from concentration camps and the killing of asylum patients (the so-called 'Euthanasia programme') in terms of their institutional history. No one was 'concentrated' in the Nazi death camps of Chełmno (which was actually not really a 'camp' in any meaningful sense), Sobibór, Bełżec, or Treblinka, where Jews (and a small number of Roma and Sinti) were sent to die. The so-called 'work Jews' held as functionaries at these camps—as carpenters, blacksmiths, and so on—to facilitate their running were few in number and also destined to die. The Holocaust has confused our understanding of concentration camps, in that the SS's camp system, as well as the many other camps in Nazi-occupied Europe run by other agencies such as the Wehrmacht, industry, or local councils, was separate from the programme known as the 'final solution to the Jewish problem' until quite late in the war and because two camps, Majdanek and Auschwitz, combined the functions of concentration camp and death camp. As we will see, the Nazi concentration camps in the strict sense were not established to murder the Jews; their history of change and, during the war, massive expansion, was primarily in response to the Nazis' wish to eradicate political and 'asocial' enemies in the first place, and to provide slave labour for the Reich later on in the context of total war. The confusion arose primarily because Holocaust survivors were found at the concentration camps liberated by the Allies in spring 1945 after having been forcibly marched westwards from camps evacuated in the face of the Soviet advance.

Following the defeat of Nazi Germany the world thought it knew what a concentration camp was. Take, for example, journalist Patrick Gordon Walker's description in his 1945 book *The Lid Lifts*, which described concentration camps as 'one of the exclusive characteristics and manifestations of our own age…one of the distinguishing marks by which you may know the twentieth century':

> What is it exactly that distinguishes in our minds a concentration camp from other forms of confinement? Barbed-wire, herded and crowded masses of humanity, the open-air, armed guards mounted on raised towers. These are the outward aspects of the concentration camp.
>
> They are the consequences of *large numbers* of opponents. That is, I think, the essential peculiarity of the concentration camp. The very large number of those whom you wish to deprive of liberty—far too many for the discipline, order and expense of prisons.
>
> When the concentration camp becomes a permanency it is the sign of a regime that knows it cannot command national support or even tolerance. It accepts the fact that very large numbers of its citizens, far beyond the normal percentage of criminals, are in irreconcilable opposition—or at any rate that these very large numbers of people must be deprived of their liberty.
>
> Together with this goes the inescapable corollary of a lowered respect for humanity—men and women are herded there who have been deprived of the elemental legal rights that clothe the human being who is still regarded as such: naked men and women.
>
> (*The Lid Lifts*, p. 65)

Although accurate in many ways, Gordon Walker missed some essential points here: these very large numbers of people are 'irreconcilable opponents' insofar as the regime in power perceives them to be, they are not necessarily people who have committed a crime. Indeed, they are highly unlikely to be criminals in any proper legal sense, although there are usually real criminals in concentration camps to give some appearance of truth to the regime's claims and—in the case of Nazi Germany at least—to aid the regime's goal of 'social cleansing'. They are 'enemies' only because the regime has defined them as such, due to some characteristic—appearance, 'race', class, political identification, religion—that the regime perceives as intolerable or threatening. They are also, most important, usually civilians (one should note that sometimes prisoners of war (POWs) or resistance fighters have also been held in concentration camps). These civilians are not armed opponents of a regime—rebels, terrorists, or insurrectionists—who have been incarcerated and are treated according to the laws of warfare. Quite to the contrary, and here is the crucial point that Gordon Walker hints at but does not explicitly set out: the inmates of concentration camps (I will try to avoid the word 'prisoners' because this connotes legal incarceration following a trial for a criminal activity) are outside the law. The nakedness to which Gordon Walker refers is their existential condition. As Agamben describes them, they are reduced to 'bare life' and held in a 'state of exception' where the law holds no sway and where they can be treated as the guards or the higher authorities choose, with no possibility of redress. They are effectively 'the dead on leave'. These are issues to which this book will return. Finally, we should note that Gordon Walker's description of the physical characteristics of a concentration camp is a description of a Nazi concentration camp. The iconic image that comes to mind is of Dachau or Buchenwald: the sealed camp, guarded by barbed wire and watchtowers, with the entrance gate with its ironic inscription: *Jedem das Seine* (to each his own) or *Arbeit macht frei* (work sets you free). But as this book will explore, a concentration camp need not look like a Nazi camp in order to qualify as such. In the far north or far east of the Soviet Union, for example, there was no need for barbed wire fences—if an inmate 'escaped', there was nowhere to go.

Importantly, Gordon Walker went on to note that the Third Reich was not the first regime to use concentration camps. But he argued that the German ones were 'basically and brutally different' from their predecessors in the Boer War, China, Spain, France, Russia, India, or Britain, where internment camps had held German civilians (many of them Jewish 'enemy aliens') in 1940. The difference, according to Gordon Walker, consisted first in their scale—'millions were interned in Germany'—and second in their purpose, which mutated, during the war, from destroying political opponents to 'the deliberate aims of extermination and dehumanization' through which 'the standards of the West were to be assaulted and undermined'.

Gordon Walker was wrong about the numbers; as we will see, far more people were incarcerated in Soviet and Chinese camps than in Nazi ones. We might also object that 'the standards of the West' had already included using concentration camps in colonial settings, and certainly included a disregard for colonial subjects' lives. But on the second point he produced an insight that goes to the heart of the problem. Describing the assault on Western civilization as 'sadism under calculating control', Gordon Walker highlighted the essential characteristic and terrifying problem of concentration camps: their rationality on the one hand and their extreme, transgressive, and savage unreality on the other. Kevin Passmore's *Fascism: A Very Short Introduction* describes fascists as people who 'demanded order in the name of revolution, and revolution in the name of order'. No wonder that the concentration camp is so firmly identified with fascism, for it might be regarded as brutality in the name of order and order in the name of brutality—but only if we bear in mind that 'brutality' here does not mean mere violence; rather it refers to a total abandonment of law and the creation of zones of exception where all manner of transgressive behaviour was permitted, a secure space away from the norms of society, where the ruling passion was 'licence'. Terror, in fact, becomes law. It is not arbitrary but imposed, as political philosopher Hannah Arendt wrote, in the name of destroying the fundamental features of humanity, eradicating spontaneity and making human beings superfluous. Arendt argued that what was so frightening about imperialism was that it created places where 'anything was permitted', where 'civilized' law and mores did not apply. Concentration camps, especially in the colonial context—and here we might consider Arendt's idea that fascism was a variety of colonialism 'come home' to Europe—were condensed versions of this licence. They are places where de facto opponents of a regime—as defined by the regime—are held indefinitely, without recourse to law, stripped of all rights, and all subjected to 'total domination'. Even though Arendt herself recognized that no regime is so 'perfect' that it can actually establish 'total domination'—'One man will always be left to tell the story'—the domination that concentration camps represent should leave us with no doubt as to the destructive capacities of the modern state.

Arendt described three types of camps, 'corresponding to three basic Western conceptions of a life after death: Hades, Purgatory, and Hell':

> To Hades correspond those relatively mild forms, once popular in even non-totalitarian countries, for getting undesirable elements of all sorts—refugees, stateless persons, the asocial and the unemployed—out of the way; as DP camps, which are nothing other than camps for persons who have become superfluous and bothersome, they have survived the war. Purgatory is represented by the Soviet Union's labor camps, where neglect is combined with chaotic forced labor. Hell in the most literal sense was embodied by those types of camps perfected by the Nazis, in which the whole of life was thoroughly and systematically organized with a view to the greatest possible torment.
>
> All three types have one thing in common: the human masses sealed off in them are treated as if they no longer existed, as if what happened to them were no longer of any interest to anybody, as if they were already dead and some evil spirit gone mad were amusing himself by stopping them for a while between life and death before admitting them to eternal peace.

(*The Origins of Totalitarianism*, p. 445)

Arendt's distinctions between the Nazi and Soviet camps are unsustainable in certain respects. Nevertheless, the distinction between Hades, Purgatory, and Hell is helpful, as we will see, even if the boundaries between them are not clear cut. This book will show that Arendt's seemingly abstract observations in fact allow us to reconsider the history of concentration camps. Although she rightly places the Nazi camps at the apex of horror, we can use her classification to see that focusing only on the Nazi camps, or taking them as exemplary of concentration camps, is to miss important points in their history. Not least, if we accept that concentration camps need not look like Dachau or Belsen, we see that in some ways we have come full circle: the camps in the Democratic Republic of Congo that were established after the Rwandan genocide remind us of the camps of the Anglo-Boer War. Concentration camps are not only products of 'mad' dictators but have a global history that belongs to the liberal West as well. Most important, Arendt's basic point about concentration camps is worth holding on to. Concentration camps are experiments in the annihilation of man. That they have existed at all is a blot on humanity; that they still exist is an indictment of our fine pretensions to universal human rights.

Chapter 2
Origins

Concentration camps existed a generation before the Third Reich proclaimed its existence, even though they might not have looked like Dachau. Where do the origins of the camps lie? Traditionally, the answer is South Africa, and one observes the same kind of peculiar British pride in being the originators of concentration camps as one sometimes encounters when discussing the occurrence of 'total' genocide in the British settler colony of Tasmania. Yet historically speaking, it is too simple to say that the British simply 'invented' concentration camps in the context of the Anglo-Boer War. First, there were precedents in Cuba and in the Philippines; but more to the point, the phenomenon of the concentration camp as it appeared in the late 19th and early 20th centuries was the logical extension of phenomena that had long characterized colonial rule: the use of reservations, of deporting population groups from their original places of residence to unsuitable locations away from the developing settler-colonial territory, and of island prisons designed to hold unwanted remnants of indigenous peoples. Quarantine and lazaret islands, such as those in Mahon harbour, leper colonies, workhouses, slavery plantations, and asylums might also be regarded as earlier precedents, if only insofar as they show that the principle of isolating groups perceived as dangerous has a long history.

The Cuban and South African camps were certainly called 'concentration camps' but we need to bear in mind that the term has, since the end of the Second World War, called to mind something different from what it originally meant. That fact means that the early camps have been exploited by particular national myth-makers, who derive satisfaction from playing on the implied suggestion that 'concentration camps' in South Africa or Cuba share similarities with those built by the Nazis. This means we need to analyse what the first concentration camps were for, how they developed, and, most crucially, how they differ from those that came later. It is important, as Iain Smith and Andreas Stucki, two historians of concentration camps in colonial settings, remind us, 'to acknowledge distinctions when the same term is used to describe widely differing phenomena in different contexts and eras'. That does not mean that there are no links to be found between camps in one place or time and another, merely that one cannot take such links for granted. Most important, the term 'concentration camp', like any other concept, means different things over time. Yet studying the early concentration camps can help us to understand how and why the camps emerged when they did and clarify the links and differences between them and the concentration camps of the fascist and communist regimes of the mid-20th century.

Prior to the existence of 'concentration camps', we can see that places of exclusion that colonial authorities set up often look, from today's perspective, like proto-concentration camps. That should not be surprising, since an institution such as a concentration camp bears similarities to many other sorts of institutions, such as military encampments, workhouses, reservations for 'natives', POW camps, and so on. Examples are easy to find. In the United States, the 1830 Indian Removal Act authorized the deportation of indigenous people from east of the Mississippi River to the as yet non-incorporated territories of the North American continent. The so-called 'Five Civilized Tribes'—the Cherokee, Choctaw,

Chickasaw, Seminole, and Creek nations—were deported, on what became known as the 'Trail of Tears', to a territory in present-day Oklahoma. The deportation itself was catastrophic for the Indians, thousands of whom died en route. But the worst would happen on arrival: of the 10,000 Creeks who were 'resettled', for example, some 3,500 died of 'bilious fevers'. The site was not a 'concentration camp' in the sense of being a guarded site of confinement; but the idea—and the reality—of dumping a 'superfluous' population group in a place where they had no connection with the land, where there were few natural resources, and where they would receive no aid from the American authorities forms part of the background to the history of the concentration camps. Other examples in the American context include the fate of the Diné (Navajo), who in 1864 were forcibly walked 300 miles from Fort Defiance, Arizona, to Bosque Redondo in New Mexico, where they were interned for four years, living in covered holes in the ground; or the Chiricahua and other western Apache peoples who were held in reservations in the 1870s and 1880s, in a disastrous policy which led to years of hardship and warfare.

In the same year as the Indian Removal Act (1830), the remaining Australian Aborigines on the island of Tasmania, who had been hunted down and killed since the start of European settlement fifty years earlier, were forcibly removed to Flinders Island. By 1838, of the 200 Aborigines sent there, only eighty remained alive. This form of segregation is not the same as holding civilians in a concentration camp, but the similarities are undeniable. Although conceived by the British rulers of Tasmania as a 'civilizing' effort, and even if the Aborigines were persuaded of the necessity of moving to Flinders Island—the alternative was to be shot on sight by settlers—the island had few resources suitable to sustain the Aborigines' lives. Although not a form of outright murder, the expulsion to Flinders Island was effectively a form of slow death and the island itself a sort of open-air camp.

Although we can see institutions which suggest that states were starting, especially in the colonial context, to 'manage' unwanted civilian populations by deporting and isolating them, the 'concentration camp' proper is usually understood as having originated in Cuba in the context of the Spanish–American War, in South Africa in the context of the Anglo-Boer War, and in the Philippines in the context of American intervention there. In each of these cases, professional European armies, which considered themselves to be fighting primitive, unworthy opponents, carried out a scorched earth policy in order to clear a rural population suspected of supporting guerrillas; this practice led to the creation of camps designed to hold this uprooted population. In the colonies, where it was easy for armies focused on means and not ends to abandon the rules of war newly set down in the 1899 Hague Laws (although these did not apply to civilians), the turn to using camps happened quickly and easily.

In Cuba, following the rebel attack on the island's sugar plantations, led by Maximo Gomez, thousands of rural workers and their families were left destitute. The rebels demanded that they should move to areas under their control but the Spanish, in response, destroyed the rural workers' crops and livestock and insisted that the population should be 're-concentrated' in areas it controlled. During the period 1896–7, the Spanish general Valeriano Weyler was responsible for moving half a million people, over a quarter of the island's population, to concentration centres, where more than 10,000 are believed to have died of starvation and disease. Although the re-concentration policy was ended in 1897, when Weyler was recalled, the majority of those held in the camps had nowhere else to go and large numbers continued to die throughout 1898.

In the Philippines, war between the Americans and the Filipinos erupted in February 1899 following the American defeat of the Spanish in 1898, as rebel leader Emilio Aguinaldo's forces demanded independence and the US opted for annexation. Defeated in formal battle, the Filipinos turned to guerrilla warfare. Under General Arthur MacArthur, in 1901–2 the Americans pursued a policy exactly along the lines they had so heavily criticized the Spanish for in Cuba: destroying dwellings and crops on south-west Luzon, ordering the killing or capturing of men found outside the towns, and forcing rural civilians into 'protected zones' in Batangas and Laguna provinces. More than 300,000 were held this way, of whom at least 10,000 died of disease.

If concentration camps first appeared in Cuba or in the Philippines, it is the camps established by the British army in South Africa that are most people's first point of reference, especially in the English-speaking world. British welfare campaigner Emily Hobhouse's condemnation of the camps as a terrible deviation from civilized human behaviour, especially her condemnation of what she called 'child murder', are widely recalled as the first recorded indictments of the evils of concentration camps. The camps—first called 'refugee camps' or 'burgher camps' and only 'concentration camps' after 1901—were set up in August 1900 and were intended to gather Boer civilians whose land and farms had been destroyed by the British army's scorched earth policy. That policy itself was the result of the ostensibly defeated Boers turning to guerrilla warfare rather than conventional battles; the camps were supposed to deprive the Boers of support and resources such as food, ammunition, and intelligence. As the number of camp inmates rose over 100,000, the British army soon found itself unable to meet the needs of so many people, with disastrous consequences (see Figure 1). But the people who found themselves in British concentration camps were not only white, as Afrikaner collective memory recalls. In fact, almost as many black Africans as Afrikaners died in the camps, even though Afrikaners appropriated the camps for their own political gain after the Anglo-Boer War. The black Africans were likely to find themselves used as a labour force, however, whereas

1. Norvals Pont camp in South Africa during the Anglo-Boer War.

the Afrikaners were also subjected to social engineering measures such as schooling for children conducted in English.

Nor were camps' inhabitants solely middle class, again as Afrikaner collective memory holds. The first camps, like that at Bloemfontein, housed destitute refugees, but as historian Elizabeth Van Heyningen says, 'by the end of 1900, and as the commandos gained strength and the British military became increasingly frustrated, the camps began to acquire a punitive function'. This sort of poor relief in the context of colonial war meant that helping the 'indigent Boer' permitted the creation of camps which soon became more forms of incarceration than assistance. Indeed, the scandalously high death rates in the camps' early months indicates a total disregard for civilian life on the part of the British army. But from the colonial authorities' point of view, especially the military, in South Africa just as in Cuba or the Philippines, such detention of civilians was justified in terms of 'clearing' the countryside of potential support for 'an evasive enemy who had resorted to guerrilla warfare'. Concentration camps held civilians but were considered an arm of military strategy, even if 'humanitarian' claims could also be made that such camps permitted civilians affected by the war to be safely housed and fed (see Box 1).

Box 1 Concentration camps in the Anglo-Boer War

The camps established by H. H. Kitchener were designed to flush out guerrillas by clearing the countryside. Their poor organization led to the deaths of some 45,000 people, about 25,000 Boers and 20,000 Africans, facts that were condemned by Emily Hobhouse among others and which have long been regarded as a stain on the British Empire. Recent research by historians such as Iain Smith and Elizabeth Van Heyningen shows that once the British proconsul Alfred Milner took charge and placed the camps under civilian control, conditions improved, that there was considerable regional variation in the camps' death rates, and that the memory of the camps has been exploited by Afrikaner nationalists. All of this more nuanced history is right and proper but it is worth bearing in mind Jonathan Hyslop's reminder that the camps' early period was disastrous. He adds:

> Of course no one should sensibly suggest that there was a moral equivalence between these institutions and the Nazi or Stalinist camps. But…the international 1896–1907 developments did mark an unprecedented level of the military organization of civilian populations. The South African camps therefore represent a form of instrumental rationality which is not without affinities to later, more totalitarian events. Indeed, the South African camps' sanitary and modernizing elements may in a sense have made them all the more pernicious, by legitimizing the camp idea internationally. It seems to me that the danger in the new literature is that in its anxiety to debunk Afrikaner nationalist ideology, it inadvertently takes on a curiously apologetic tone on behalf of the British military and administrative machines.
>
> ('The Invention of the Concentration Camp', p. 260 n. 33)

As Elizabeth Van Heyningen notes, it is unhelpful that

> The term 'concentration camp' has acquired far more terrible
> connotations since the Second World War and, for some people, the
> distinction between the South African and Nazi camps has blurred,
> contributing to a belief that the British camps were genocidal.

Still, as she goes on, 'no one chooses to be a refugee and the term
always implies deprivation and suffering. The polemics of war are
unhelpful in understanding the history of the camps.'

The other colonial context in which concentration camps
appeared was German South-West Africa (today Namibia). In the
context of the Herero and Nama War (1904–7) what is today
widely regarded as the first genocide of the 20th century took
place, with some 65,000 of the 80,000-strong Herero population
murdered or driven into the desert to die of thirst. At the end of
the war against the Herero, the German colonial force established
what it called *Konzentrationslager* or *Gefangenenkraale* for the
surviving Herero, brutal camps in which the death rate was 45 per
cent, or twice as high as the British camps in South Africa (see
Figure 2). Given that the term *Konzentrationslager* had been used
in German, up to that point, to refer to the British camps in South
Africa, it is clear that the British experience in their guerrilla war
was regarded as some kind of guide by the Germans. Although
similar to the Cuban and South African cases in that the German
army regarded guerrilla warfare as intolerable, there was a crucial
difference in that the South-West African camps were conceived as
pacification and 'punishment' camps for an already defeated enemy
who could henceforth be used for forced labour and not as a means
of isolating civilians in the context of a guerrilla war. As a result,
the harder attitudes already prevailing among the colonial rulers
meant that from the start these camps endured a harsher rule.

The most notorious case was Shark Island (Haifischinsel), off the
Namibian coast, to which 1,800 Herero were deported after the

2. Shark Island, German South-West Africa (Namibia).

war. One eye-witness, a German missionary from Lüderitz Bay, noted that the Hereros' mistreatment whilst at work, the lack of fresh food, and the raw sea climate quickly weakened them.

> Even more than these evils, their isolation on the furthest corner of Shark Island contributed to the eradication of the people's will to live. They became gradually apathetic towards their misery. They were separated from the outside world by three high barbed wire fences.

By the time the camp was transferred to the mainland in April 1907, on the orders of Ludwig von Estorff, the new head of the

Schutztruppe (colonial army), only 245 Herero were still alive, of whom only twenty-five were able to work. These figures appear to justify historian Isabel Hull's claim that the German army's military culture—which required maintaining prestige in the face of 'savages', a quick and absolute victory, and a low level of priority to logistical questions—proved fatal for Germany's colonial subjects once they took up arms against their 'masters'.

The fact that the Herero were subjected to forced labour only hastened their demise, even if the decision to put them to work brought a slight increase in food rations. They were primarily forced to work building railway lines. Private firms also made use of the Herero as forced labourers, for example the shipping firm Woermann, as well as small local firms, who paid a fee to the camp administrators for each person they took. In general, however, the dispute between different German military leaders as to whether the Herero should be used for labour or should be left to die in the camps made no difference to their massive death rate. Although there were no death camps in German South-West Africa, the concentration camps there brought about an annihilation through neglect and thus they contributed enormously to the German reshaping of South-West African society.

These colonial camps were 'concentration camps', then, because that is what those who established them called them. Yet they were not uniform and, in the case of Cuba at least, it is questionable whether the term 'concentration camp' really applies, given its later 20th-century connotations. Why did they emerge at this point, and what contributed to their steady radicalization? The first thing to note is the professionalization of European armies in the late 19th century. This professionalization paradoxically permitted intensified violence against civilians because, as historian Jonathan Hyslop argues, it led armies to regard other armies as worthy of respect and subject to rules when taken prisoner, but permitted the development of 'a doctrine of military necessity as justifying extreme violence' when dealing with civilians or those figured as 'irregular troops'. Concentration camps emerged as weapons of war and became tools of total war even though, paradoxically, they were used to incarcerate not enemy combatants but supposedly seditious civilians. Particularly in the colonies, where racial assumptions of native inferiority and European superiority were taken for granted, any threat to this way of thinking was intolerable. Second, the spread of new technologies of communication at the turn of the 20th century facilitated the easy spread of information with respect to all aspects of life, including military and carceral techniques. Third, and of greater importance for understanding the radicalization of concentration camps, the brutal experience of the First World War, the creation of nationalizing states in the aftermath of the demise of the old European empires, a development that occurred at the same time as the European overseas empires were also at their zenith, gave states a major spur to conceive of widespread incarceration of civilians in terms of their own security or 'self-defence'.

Particularly during the Great War, notions of states' 'self-defence' received a boost through the holding of large numbers of POWs and the internment of 'enemy' civilians, procedures which set important precedents for the new nation states. The whole of France was legally placed in a state of siege by President Poincaré in August 1914, a condition which remained in effect until 12 October 1919, and during which time the National Assembly became nothing more than a mouthpiece for rule by decree. Where states of exception formerly existed in colonial spaces, now they were being created in Europe; they were enablers of mass incarceration.

Between 1914 and 1918 between eight and nine million soldiers were held as POWs, about one in every nine men in uniform. The camps in which they were held were not concentration camps—not because they were too pleasant or comfortable but because they held soldiers and should thus be classed as POW camps. Their significance here is that they indicated a newfound ability to transport and maintain ever larger numbers of people on the part of modern states. Or more accurately, they indicate that states lacked or chose to restrict the ability to maintain large numbers of people. Over 9 per cent of the 2.11 million Habsburg POWs in Russian captivity died in the camps, and another 9 per cent were missing. Nearly 10 per cent of the 158,000 German soldiers in Russian captivity died; more than 72,000 of the 1.4 million Russian POWs held by the Central Powers died according to contemporary German estimates—the true figure is likely to be higher; nearly 20 per cent of Italian POWs (over 92,000 of 468,000) died in Austrian captivity.

These figures reflect the simple fact that food was withheld from POWs, that they were often forced to work in areas where they came under fire—contrary to the 1907 Hague Convention—and that they received inadequate clothing and shelter. One British soldier held in Sennelager camp in September 1914 described it as 'an open field enclosed with wire...there were no tents or covering in it of any kind. There were about 2,000 prisoners in it—all British. We lay on the ground with only one blanket for three men.' Italian POWs were marched to camps whose names—Mauthausen, Theresienstadt—immediately indicate the link between POW camps and later concentration camps. One Italian POW wrote home: 'We are treated like animals; with our tattered shoes we resemble tramps. I hope this damned war is over soon, or else we will die in Austria.' Yet none fared worse in Austrian captivity than the Serbs who, according to the Italian high command, were kept caged like animals and fed scraps, leading them to conclude that 'Austria intends to destroy the [Serb] race.' As historian of the POW camps Heather Jones notes, in the First World War the

> prisoner of war camp began the conflict as a means of ensuring that the captured enemy combatant was kept away from rejoining the battlefield fight; in other words, with a purely military function; it ended the war as a sophisticated system of state control and as a

laboratory for new ways of managing mass confinement, forced labour and new forms of state-military collaboration.

Even more significant for later developments was the internment of civilians during the First World War, and not only in Europe. In 1915, in a move that had enormous ramifications for the rest of the 20th century and beyond, France revoked the status of naturalized citizens from people of 'enemy origin'. Belgium, Italy, Austria, and Germany soon followed suit, with the result that the idea became widely accepted that one could be stripped of one's nationality and reduced to statelessness and thus deprived of the benefit of law—this being long before the UN Refugee Convention, of course. British civilians in Germany, for example, were held in the Engländerlager Ruhleben near Berlin. In total, by the end of the war, some 111,879 'enemy civilians' were in German internment. 24,255 German, Austrian, and Hungarian civilians were still interned in Britain at the same point, October 1918. The Austro-Hungarians deported French and Belgian citizens for forced labour and Italian citizens of the Austro-Hungarian Empire for being 'out of place': they were either interned or deported to Italy. From 20 May 1915 they were held in what were called 'concentration camps', one of which, at Steinklamm, the Italians referred to as the 'Campo della morte' (camp of death). The internees were treated very harshly, forced to work for little pay, and received inadequate food supplies. The Italian royal commission of investigation noted, in fact, that the 'really tragic characteristic of these concentration camps was the hunger' and, in the face of large numbers of deaths, especially of children, claimed that the Austrians intended to 'destroy or reduce to a small number the Italian race on its territories'. The Austrians also rounded up some 7,000 so-called 'Russophiles' in eastern Galicia and Bukovina and deported them to the Thalerhof camp near Graz, where nearly 1,500 died. In the colonies, German priests and civilians in Togo and Cameroon were rounded up and interned first in Dahomey and later in Algeria and Morocco, and in British East Africa German civilians were deported to camps in India. Whether undertaken out of fear of 'fifth columnists', as reprisal actions, or in order to obtain forced labourers, the scale of civilian internment during the war was far greater than anything that had been witnessed before.

Most notable, however, were the huge numbers of refugees created by the Russian Revolution of 1917 (about 1.5 million), by the Ottoman attacks on Armenians (about one million), as well by the collapse of the European empires at the end of the war, which affected among others Greeks, Turks, and Bulgarians. Within the Russian Empire itself, before the Bolshevik Revolution the Tsarist regime deported some 300,000 Lithuanians, 250,000 Latvians, 200,000 Germans, 500,000 Jews, and 743,000 Poles from the western border regions. As a group of Russian Germans claimed: 'We didn't want to move, we were chased away...we were forced to burn our homes and crops, we weren't allowed to take our cattle with us, we weren't even allowed to return to our homes to get some money.' By mid-1916, in Russia's larger cities refugees made up more than 10 per cent of the population; in Kharkov it was 25 per cent and in Samara 30 per cent. There were philanthropic efforts to help them, but these were insufficient to counter the power of a nationalist language of 'floods', 'swarms', 'deluges', and other biblical disasters, which quickly became associated with refugees. *The Times*, for example, described Belgian refugees in Britain as 'a peaceful invasion', and Russian commentators used even more colourful terms such as 'lava' or 'avalanche'. These population movements saw emergency accommodation being created in schools, factories, barracks, monasteries, and so on, and the creation of refugee camps for the first time on European soil. The refugees were not always grateful, however. Belgians in Britain, for example, were constrained by the Aliens Restriction Act (4 August 1914), confining them to specific parts of the country; they complained that this amounted to being held in a 'concentration camp'.

These developments together—the war itself, the large numbers of civilians and combatants being held in camps, the existence of huge groups of refugees, and the creation of states of exception in European polities—contributed to a rapidly changing political environment, one in which whole groups could fall under suspicion and find themselves subject to states' paranoias and fears, which mushroomed at this time. Klaus Mühlhahn claims that

> The temporary internment of displaced and dislocated groups and POWs in the wake of the war together with the politicisation of citizenship and nationality and the temporary suspension of regular legal procedures provided the conditio sine qua non that facilitated the emergence of concentration camps on the European continent.

This might be somewhat overstating the case—other conditions were also relevant, not least the colonial precedents—but his claim is a useful rejoinder to those who only remember the South African camps and forget that within Europe itself camps for civilians existed several decades before the Nazis came to power. The First World War generated the interventionist state, threatened the rule of law, intensified notions of national belonging, and raised fears about civilians and citizens who were 'out of place'—all of which resulted in the creation of camps. Twenty years later, and despite the Geneva Convention of 1929, the same phenomenon would reappear as 'enemy aliens'—including German and Austrian Jewish refugees—were interned on the Isle of Man in the UK, as camps opened in the south of France for refugees from the Spanish Civil War, and as similar sites appeared around the world. Camps for the stateless, the non-naturalized, and simply those rendered suspect by the dominance of nationalist ways of thinking had become normalized.

These European developments indicate a link between colonial rule and the radicalization of state actions in Europe. But perhaps the most radical indication of the way in which concentration camps were changing during the period of the Great War is to be found in the Ottoman Empire, where some historians talk of concentration camps being used in the genocide of the Ottoman Armenians. In this context, one can clearly see the ways in which 'concentration camps' could rapidly drift into something altogether more terrible in the context of total war. These camps were often holding pens during the process of deportation of Armenians from the Turkish interior to the deserts of Syria. At Aleppo, for example, large numbers of deportees were forced to camp along the railway tracks outside of the city so as not to overcrowd the city itself. 'As a result,' Hilmar Kaiser writes, 'new concentration camps emerged for deportees in transit.' One of them was Katma (or Ghatma). One witness, Vahram Daderian, described it thus in September 1915:

> The sea of people with coaches, horses, donkeys, mules and people are filled in all direction [sic]. The atmosphere is filled with a deafening sound of cursing, crying, and sighing. Skeleton arms are stretched out everywhere, asking for a piece of bread…There is a terrible stink that tears everyone's nose. Everywhere is covered with unburned, rotten human waste, corpses etc. Besides that, ten thousand people have left their filth, and have contaminated the whole area, and it is not possible not to choke. Holding our nose and covering our eyes, we proceeded among these corpses and garbage, and after a while we stopped at a place at the end of the tent city, which was specially prepared for us.

(cited in Kaiser, At the Crossroads, p. 19)

Or, as Elise Hagobian Taft put it in her memoir *Rebirth* (1981), describing Katma in December 1915:

> The sight before me was horrible beyond description. Hundreds and hundreds of swollen bodies lay in the mud and puddles of rain water, some half-buried, others floating eerily in rancid pools, together with rotted bodies and heaps of human refuse accumulated during the week-long rain. Some victims—only the upper torsos emerging from the mud and puddles—were breathing their last. The stench rose to

the heavens. It was nauseating beyond belief. The scene was like a
huge cesspool laid bare and made to stink even more under a hot sun.

(cited in Kaiser, *At the Crossroads*, p. 21)

Or finally, in Naomie Ouzounian's description, written in 1982:

The 'camp' where hundreds of thousands had already been thrown
together was a narrow strip of the desert, surrounded by bare hills.
The hot, humid air was filled with the stench of human refuse and
decaying unburied bodies. I couldn't breathe, oh, if only I could
take a deep breath! The name of this hell was Ghatma. 'Dear Lord,
I hope there is no Ghatma in the hereafter, and if there is one,
forgive my sins and do not condemn me to it', I prayed.

(cited in Kaiser, *At the Crossroads*, pp. 21–2)

Kaiser goes on to talk of the 'world of the death camps' as the
genocide became more coordinated and ferocious in 1916. Other
historians agree, Ron Suny claiming that the 'concentration
camps' at Tel-Abiad, Ras al Ayn, Mamureh, Katma, and Aleppo
'were way stations toward extermination. They were death camps.'
Taner Akçam too says of the 'concentration camps' of Aleppo that
'the appalling sanitary and humanitarian conditions turned these
into death camps'. Is this a metaphor? Ouzounian talks of the
'camp' at Katma in inverted commas, suggesting it was not really a
camp in the sense of our working definition so much as a forced
encampment where the deportees were left to fend for themselves.
The language of 'death camps' here derives from the Nazi period,
as does Suny's claim that the name of Der el Zor 'reverberates
today with the final solution of the Armenian question'; the
tragedy of the Armenian genocide is by no means diminished if
we suggest that the term is not wholly appropriate. What we see
in the Armenian genocide is something part way between the
colonial dumping grounds and the Nazi death camps. People were
not murdered on arrival at Der el Zor as at Treblinka; but they
were separated off from the rest of the population and abandoned

to die. The difference pertains solely to the institutional history of the concentration camp, the different logics of the perpetrators' world views, and the means of technology at their disposal, not to the value of the lives of the victims in either case.

Over time, as we have seen in this chapter, concentration camps emerged not only as institutions developed by different states—which suggests that they tell us something about modern nation-state building—but as sites whose creators were radicalizing them in a logical fashion as the first half of the 20th century became increasingly violent. European racism, military culture, more rapid forms of communication, and increasingly available print media all contributed to the global diffusion of the idea of the concentration camp. Russian military officials, for example, first used the term *konsentratsionnyi lager* during the Anglo-Boer War and the Bolsheviks quickly revived the term after the 1917 revolution. In Germany, the term *Konzentrationslager* was first adopted from the British camps in South Africa as the designation for the camps set up to hold the Herero in German South-West Africa. After the war, in 1921, the term was again officially used to designate two camps, in Cottbus-Sielow and Stargard in Pomerania, established on the sites of former POW camps in order to hold 'unwanted foreigners', primarily 'Ostjuden', that is Jews from Eastern Europe. In Asia, the Japanese established their first concentration camp, Zhong Ma prison camp, in the village of Beiyinhe, about 100 km south of Harbin. The numbers of Chinese and Korean 'bandits' held there was small—about 500—but the significance of Zhong Ma was that the inmates were used as human guinea pigs in germ warfare experiments. It was thus the forerunner of the Japanese Special Unit 731, which between 1937 and 1945 carried out experiments on human beings at its facility in Ping Fan, near Harbin, as well as at sites in Nanjing and Changchun. Many other 'corrective labour camps', as the Japanese called them, were established across Manchuria in the 1930s.

The Chinese too, under the Nationalist Government (1938–49), set up concentration camps for political enemies, assisted in the process by the Germans and the Americans. Among them was General Alexander von Falkenhausen, a friend of Lothar von Trotha, the man responsible for suppressing the Herero in German South-West Africa, who advised the Chinese on the basis of German and British experience in the colonies, as well as his own role in putting down the Boxer uprising. The Guomindang was also advised by American officers. Stationed near the Chongqing prison camp, they helped to train nationalist Chinese agents in interrogation techniques. Although the European model of camps acquired a certain 'Confucian' twist in its Chinese variant—through the names of buildings, the designation of inmates as 'people in self-cultivation', and through the language of 'thought reform', for example—it is clear that the Chinese camp system also owed something to precedents in the European colonies and in Europe itself. In the interwar years, then, we see that concentration camps across the world appeared principally as an aspect of the development of modern states but also, to a more limited extent, on the basis of transnational exchanges of information and technology. As Dai Li, head of the Juntong or intelligence service, put it in a 1966 recollection: 'It is correct, we had concentration camps; but I think that in times of war every state has organized similar institutions, detaining political prisoners as well as enemies and spies who do harm to national security.'

In the global context of colonial settlement and warfare, the rise of mass politics in Europe, the challenges to European empires, and the emergence of new, homogenizing nation states in the aftermath of the Great War—itself an occasion for radical approaches to internment of civilians and combatants alike—concentration camps became firmly established as part of the state's carceral repertoire. According to Hyslop, the colonial camps, in comparison with what came later, 'were very limited affairs in terms of the levels of guarding, violence and discipline to which the prisoners were subjected'. Nor were they entirely isolated from legal and civilian criticisms: Kitchener's plans to expand his remit were blocked by the Cabinet, and in Germany von Trotha's 'war of annihilation' created considerable scandal in parliament and in the press. Nevertheless, the idea of the concentration camp as a holding pen for superfluous or undesirable people who could be excluded from the realm of domestic and international law had, by the end of the First World War, become accepted as a technique of rule. The adoption of concentration camps by the Japanese in Manchuria and the Chinese nationalists in their attempt to put down communism makes the point clearly. But nowhere would this be more evident than in the Soviet Union, in Nazi Germany, and, after 1939, in Nazi-occupied Europe. It is to these two regimes, Nazi and Soviet, and the extraordinary world of camps they produced that we will turn next.

Chapter 3
The Third Reich's world of camps

'Certainly, anyone who had dealt with the Nazis outside a camp did not expect anything good inside one,' writes Boris Pahor, the Slovenian former inmate of four Nazi camps. The truth of his dictum was evident from the moment the Nazis came to power. In March 1933, Stefan Lorant, the editor of the *Münchner Illustrierte Presse* and a Hungarian citizen, was arrested and held in prison in 'protective custody' for six and a half months. When he tried to understand what was happening he alighted on the notion that for millions of Germans 'Adolf Hitler is the deliverer from "shame and disgrace"'. Lorant believed that ordinary Germans fell under a kind of spell, that the 'time was ripe for a messiah—even a false one'. Lorant found himself one of the early victims of this messianism—those who did not fit the image of the new Germany were to be ruthlessly removed, irrespective of anything they had or had not actually done. As Lorant put it, under the terms of 'protective custody', 'We have been locked up for crimes which we have not committed, but which we might commit as soon as we are free.'

Lorant's story was, in 1933, and still in 1935 when his book was published, a brutal and shocking one, but it marked only the start of Nazi Germany's creation of an ever-expanding extrajudicial system of exclusion and incarceration. From the prison in Munich, some of the inmates were sent to Dachau, and it was already more than clear to the men that however unpleasant their cells were, Dachau was not a place they wanted to see, since 'Those who are incarcerated there stand only the slenderest chance of ever coming out again.' In fact, contrary to Lorant's perception, most early inmates of the Nazi camps were released. Lorant, shocked by being set free in September 1933 as suddenly as he had been arrested, found himself on a Munich street with daily life going on around him: 'Calm, peace, and order reigned.' 'And yet,' he wrote, 'a few yards away, hundreds, thousands of innocent people were locked up in cells, a few yards away from the peaceful scene before me the victims of National-Socialism were torturing themselves and being tortured.' Ten years after Lorant's book appeared, this description of Nazi 'protective custody' would seem tame. Yet in the legal notion of 'Schutzhaft', or protective custody, is to be found the specifically German root of the Nazi concentration camps.

Lorant's book was a bestselling book in the UK, especially when it was reprinted as a Penguin Special in 1940, but it was by no means alone. Many books described the Third Reich's prisons and concentration camps in the 1930s in Western Europe and the US, the accounts of incarceration with titles such as *Rubber Truncheon*, *Men Crucified*, or *Dachau: The Nazi Hell* selling very well. Likewise, many journalistic and scholarly analyses of the Third Reich published in the 1930s and 1940s sought to explain the phenomenon of the camps, notable examples being those by Hermann Rauschning, Calvin B. Hoover, Stephen H. Roberts, F. A. Voigt, Aurel Kolnai, and Franz Neumann. As well as these condemnatory accounts, however, more sympathetic appraisals, such as *Daily Mail* journalist G. Ward Price's *I Know These Dictators* (1937), explained that the 'German nation' conceived of itself as in a 'state of siege' and justified the 'vigorous' use of concentration camps as necessary in the struggle against 'ruthless and treacherous' adversaries. 'Great capital,' wrote Ward Price,

> has been made by the enemies of Germany out of the
> concentration-camps, just as it was made by the enemies of Britain

out of alleged abuses in the concentration-camps in South Africa during the Boer War. In both cases gross and reckless exaggerations were made. That there would have been far more cruelty in Germany if the Communists had been the guardians instead of the inmates of the concentration-camps is proved by the horrors that went on wherever Bolshevists have gained the upper hand.

Ward Price's account shows how right Lorant was when he wrote that foreign visitors to Germany 'are only allowed to see the surface of things. Which of them has any knowledge of the life in the concentration camps, in the prisons, or in the barracks of the SA?'

In fact, just as British or American readers could learn a good deal about the early Nazi camps, so too could Germans, for the Nazis advertised Dachau and Sachsenhausen in the press (along the lines of Figure 3) as proof of their resolve to 're-educate' and 'cleanse' Germany. The SS journal *Das Schwarze Korps*, for example, ran an article on 13 February 1936 in which images of concentration camp inmates were accompanied by the following explanation: 'This is a collection of race traitors, sexual degenerates, and common criminals who have spent the better part of their lives behind bars and other individuals who have cast themselves outside the bounds of the national community with their conduct and only three years ago were still being coddled by psychoanalysts and defense attorneys as "victims of bourgeois society"'. Just a few weeks earlier the *Völkischer Beobachter* argued that protective custody was a vital function of the concentration camps. 'The main core of the inmates of the concentration camps,' it claimed, 'are those Communist and Marxist functionaries who, as experience shows, would immediately resume their struggle against the state if set free.' As the camp system expanded, so the claim not to know about it became ever more implausible.

Early post-war accounts reveal that what had been learned in the 1930s no longer made sense, perhaps because what was discovered

3. Inmates performing slave labour, 28 July 1938.

at Belsen, Dachau, and Buchenwald did not correspond to the
earlier accounts, in which brutality was much in evidence but not
terror and human destruction on an unimaginable scale. Neither
shocked accounts of random violence nor apologetic explications
of supposedly justifiable retribution in the first years after the

Nazis came to power came close to descriptions of the camps discovered by the Allies in 1945, where filth and depravity reigned. The first post-war studies of the concentration camps such as David Rousset's (*L'univers concentrationnaire*, translated as *A World Apart*), Eugen Kogon's (*Der SS-Staat*, translated as *The Theory and Practice of Hell*), Bruno Bettelheim's (*The Informed Heart*), and, to some extent, Hannah Arendt's (*The Origins of Totalitarianism*) did not stress the 'death camps' in ways that we do now, but they placed an emphasis on 'the camp' (in French *les camps* became the shorthand for the whole system of Nazi rule, epitomized in Alain Resnais's 1955 film *Night and Fog*), which made them stand as a synecdoche for totalitarian rule as such. 'The camp', though it was historically uninformed and analytically vague, was an ethical call to resist evil in the post-war world, to 'write for the world of the living' as Arendt put it about Rousset and Kogon.

The Nazi camps—perhaps because more was known about them than the Soviets', but perhaps too because of the nature of the Nazis' ambitions—gave rise to the idea that concentration camps were not just tools of pacification during warfare, as in South Africa. They represented, rather, a new form of social existence and stood as embodiments in miniature of the totalitarian systems as such. 'From the detached point of view of descriptive sociology, a concentration camp represents a strangely unique social situation,' wrote E. K. Bramstedt in his 1945 book *Dictatorship and Political Police*. Sociologists and philosophers have continued to describe the Nazi camps in such terms. Wolfgang Sofsky, for example, describes them as 'laboratories of violence', Maja Suderland as a 'distorted image' of society outside the camps. Others have sought to explain 'values and violence in Auschwitz' (Anna Pawełczyńska), the elimination of the 'life-world' in the camps (Edith Wyschogrod), moral life in the concentration camps (Tzvetan Todorov), or its opposite, 'choiceless choice' in the camps (Lawrence Langer). Yet in the study of the Nazi camps we are always confronted with a dilemma: there is a prosaic way of describing them, usually undertaken by historians. This involves explaining the origins and development of the camps as part of Himmler's expanding SS, which gradually grew into a state within a state in the Third Reich; examining the operation of the camps—the guards, command structures, architecture and planning, work commandos, violence and punishment, and resistance—and showing how the camps changed over time, until they reached the massive operation of late 1944/early 1945 of main camps surrounded by many slave labour sub-camps. From this point of view, the Nazis' vicious destruction of political enemies and their attempt to 'clean up' society by eliminating 'asocials' and other 'undesirables' seems historically explicable, though shocking.

On the other hand, the air of madness that surrounds the camps means that such historical or sociological approaches reach a point where their explanatory power runs out. This is where the Nazi camp system intersects with the Holocaust. Even leaving out the 'pure' death camps from our purview, the camps at Auschwitz—overshadowed as they were by the continual presence and threat of the gas chambers—present a bizarre phenomenon. But probably the most difficult to comprehend from the point of view of the camps' putative purposelessness occurs at the very end of their existence: the dead mingled with the living in their tens of thousands at Belsen, the naked, emaciated survivors in Ebensee, the 'living skeletons' of Dachau and Buchenwald—these are the images of the Nazi camps that seared themselves into the world's consciousness in the newsreels of 1945. Here Hannah Arendt's point from 1950 that the concentration camps could not be understood within the frameworks of social scientific categories as they existed at that time remains fundamental: whether in law, philosophy, sociology, or history, what categories of thought, what explanatory frameworks of human behaviour can account for this phenomenon? (See Box 2.) It is hard to escape the feeling that whatever we say about the concentration camps, there is something that we just do not understand—a feeling that many

Box 2 Hannah Arendt (1906–71)

Already in 1946, Arendt had written about the Nuremberg Trial to her mentor, friend, and confidant Karl Jaspers, that the 'Nazi crimes explode the limits of the law'. In 1950 she was making basically the same point about the concentration camps: our systems of thought lack the categories necessary to take the full measure of what the Nazis had done. In *Origins of Totalitarianism* (first edn. 1951), Arendt tried to provide a systematic account which combined empirical information about the camps—their origin and administration—with philosophical reflection on their meaning, arguing that the camps were a form of 'total domination' whose only real purpose was that of 'making men superfluous'. Along with several other early post-war writers, Arendt therefore set the framework and terms of debate for representing the Holocaust which continue to this day.

survivors and commentators have also articulated: 'know what has happened, do not forget, and at the same time never will you know', as Maurice Blanchot wrote.

In 1948, American journalist Isaac Rosenfeld articulated a fear that has persisted ever since:

> We still don't understand what happened to the Jews of Europe, and perhaps we never will. There have been books, magazine and newspaper articles, eyewitness accounts, letters, diaries, documents certified by the highest authorities on the life in ghettos and concentration camps, slave factories and extermination centers under the Germans. By now we know all there is to know. But it hasn't helped; we still don't understand.
>
> (*Preserving the Hunger*, pp. 129–30)

For some, the attempt to historicize the Holocaust—by, for example, writing the history of the concentration camps in the historian's dispassionate style—is a kind of horror: footnotes objectify and belittle the suffering of human beings. It would be arrogant to dismiss this feeling as nothing more than sentimental moralizing. Nevertheless, if we want to understand at least something of how the Nazis realized their apocalyptic dystopia then the tools of the historian must be used along with those of novelists and poets. When we go on to consider that they have continued to scar the globe since 1945, the academic study of concentration camps clearly remains doubly justified.

Let us turn then to the history of the Nazi camps. In many respects the global prehistory of the concentration camps (as outlined in Chapter 2) does not help much; as Arendt noted in a criticism of Kogon's book, these are only 'apparent historical precedents'. Yet Arendt's assertion might be too easy to accept. Is there really a gulf between the Nazi system which made concentration camps the embodiment of Nazi 'values' and the use of concentration camps in the Boer War or in the internment of Spanish Civil War fighters in France? Are there not quite obvious continuities when one looks at the POW and civilian internment camps of the First World War, the concentration camps of German South-West Africa, and, especially, at the Armenian genocide?

The Nazi camps were initially set up on a relatively unorganized basis. The earliest 'proper' camps were Dachau and Oranienburg, later Sachsenhausen, camps which attracted a great deal of attention, including from the foreign press. They were places which served the purpose of ensuring that the Nazi suppression of political opposition was appreciated by the regime's enemies, a process which worked swiftly and brutally. This is why only two of the SS's six original concentration camps, Dachau and Lichtenburg, were in operation at the end of 1937. When Buchenwald was established in that same year, it was not, as is often assumed, because of the later predominance of communists among the prisoner functionaries, a camp for political prisoners; these had already been dealt with in the first two years of Nazi rule. Rather it was a camp primarily for 'asocials' and other 'Aryans' who refused to accommodate themselves to Nazism, including Jehovah's Witnesses, the 'work shy', habitual criminals, and homosexuals. Their numbers were small: there were just 7,750 men in Dachau, Sachsenhausen, and Buchenwald at the end of 1937. It was the presence of such people which led to the latter camp finding its bucolic name ('beech forest'). The logical name would have been Ettersberg, since that is where the camp is located, but as Theodor Eicke, the Inspector of Concentration Camps, wrote to Heinrich Himmler, head of the SS and Chief of the German Police, in July 1937, that name 'cannot be used' because of the Ettersberg's association with Goethe. Eicke's objection was not that Goethe's name ought not to be brought together with a concentration camp, but that his revered name should not be associated with the rejects of the *Volksgemeinschaft* ('people's community').

The point is important because it reminds us that the SS camps were initially used for the purposes of crafting the racial community and eliminating political opponents, real and imagined. The expansion of the camp system in 1938—by the end of June 1938 there were about 24,000 inmates, mostly 'asocials' and other outsiders and Austrian political prisoners, in all the SS's concentration camps—was a result of the growth in Himmler's power and his plans to expand the SS empire. The change is signalled in the administration of the camps, which were run at first by the Inspectorate of Concentration Camps (IKL) until 1942 and then by the SS's Business Administration Main Office (WVHA), a name which suggests Himmler's aspirations. The camps were changing all the time in terms of their number, prominence, and make-up of the victims. But they also remained constant in their aim of terrorizing the people the Nazis named as their enemies. It is hardly surprising that one former inmate called the camps 'schools for murder' where bestiality was systematically trained as a logical preparation for the most merciless of wars.

This process of terror was stepped up a gear in 1938 as Jews and other groups were interned in large numbers. Before the November pogrom (9–10 November 1938, popularly remembered as 'Kristallnacht'), Jews were among the concentration camp inmates, usually as political prisoners. As Jews they were subjected to especially rough treatment but after 1938 Jews targeted as such made up a consistently high proportion of the camps' inmates. Just as this attack on the Jews presaged the large-scale persecution to come, so the camp system began rapidly to expand just before the start of the war. Large numbers of Czechs, veterans of the Spanish Civil War, and, especially, Poles boosted the numbers of camp inmates in 1940, which rose to 53,000, and new camps began to open, such as Auschwitz. The latter was neither originally a camp specifically for Jews nor a death camp, but was designed to hold Polish political prisoners.

The invasion of the Soviet Union in June 1941 brought about another expansion of the camp system, with notable camps built at Lublin (Majdanek) and Stutthof. Some 38,000 Soviet 'commissars' were murdered in operation 14f14 in 1941/2 and over the course of the war some three million Soviet POWs died in German captivity. In September 1942 there were about 110,000 camp inmates; this number shot up to 224,000 a year later, 524,286 a year after that, and over 700,000 by the start of 1945, as the SS desperately tried to substitute forced labour for the shortcomings of the Third Reich's war economy. New camps, such as Mittelbau-Dora where V2 rockets were built, suddenly emerged and grew into huge, brutal factories where workers, instead of being productive in any economically meaningful sense, died in large numbers. Such huge numbers meant that far from being hidden from view, 'concentration camps in public spaces' became the norm and 'the camp world invaded everyday life as never before' (Gellately). The Buchenwald sub-camp of Magda, for example, was on the edge of Magdeburg-Rothensee, whose residents, historian Nikolaus Wachsmann reminds us, 'looked straight into the camp, while their children played next to the electric fence'.

Once again, one needs to distinguish, at least at first, between the SS concentration camps such as Buchenwald, Dachau, and Sachsenhausen, and, later, Neuengamme, Ravensbrück, Mauthausen, Stutthof, and Gross-Rosen, which were designed to brutalize the inmates, and at which death was common, and the death camps—Chełmno, Bełżec, Sobibór, and Treblinka—which were pure killing facilities, built in 1941–2, and which were not administered as part of the regular concentration camp system. The exceptions were Majdanek and Auschwitz, which by 1942 combined the functions of concentration and death camps and, especially at Auschwitz, also had massive slave labour operations attached. As well as being the primary site of the genocide of the Roma and Sinti (Gypsies), about one million Jews were murdered in the gas chambers at Auschwitz-Birkenau. Transit camps and labour camps associated with the administration of the Holocaust were also established, such as Herzogenbusch in the Netherlands. The difference between all these sorts of camps was not very widely understood during the war. This lack of clarity, combined with the chaos of the end of the war which brought the different camps crashing together, contributed to the confusion about the geography and operation of the Holocaust for years after the war's end. With the exception of Auschwitz and Majdanek, it was only late in the war that the systematic murder of Europe's Jews became entangled with the wider history of the concentration camps.

For the inmates, life in the concentration camps was brutal and is often depicted in crude Darwinian terms as a struggle for survival. Although there are many recorded instances of assistance and mutual aid amongst inmates in the camps, survival required more than luck. 'In the camps,' wrote Joop Zwart, a prominent Dutch political prisoner in Belsen in a testimony of 1958, 'the conditions there could not be measured with the moral standards of a free society.' This individualistic disregard for others might have enabled some to survive, but it also hindered the survival of the many, and there are, contrary to Zwart's claims, many instances of survivors testifying to the importance of being part of a pair, small group, or 'substitute family'. Zwart claimed that

> Nobody could afford to help first somebody else with a thing he
> himself needed most. Still, with more solidarity among the prisoners
> it is my conviction that many more thousands could have been
> saved. But it seemed as if the people in the camps did their very best
> to shed their best qualities as quickly as possible for their very worst
> qualities. So not only envy, but betrayal and worse, reigned.

This harsh judgement certainly tells us something about how the camps functioned, though Zwart omitted to mention that these conditions were not those of the inmates' own making. If they did not live up to the standards of decent behaviour, we might remember that this was one of the consequences of the camps the Nazis intended.

One of the main confusions in our understanding of the Nazi camps concerns the role played by work. The term 'annihilation through labour' (*Vernichtung durch Arbeit*) is widely understood to refer to a deliberately conceived Nazi policy. In fact, concentration camp inmates had been used for forced labour from the camps' early days. Later in the war, when foreign forced and volunteer labourers (of whom there were already some twelve million in Germany) proved insufficient, concentration camp labour was used more readily because of the shortages in manpower from which the German economy was suffering. It was at this point—autumn 1944—that large numbers of sub-camps appeared. Gross-Rosen, for example, had over a hundred sub-camps by the end of 1944 and, with nearly 77,000 inmates, held some 11 per cent of the total concentration camp population.

Where concentration camp inmates—as opposed to forced labourers—were forced to work, this was only ever a temporary measure designed to extract as much value as possible out of inmates before their deaths. Particularly for Jews, work was only meant as a brief interlude, a necessary evil. It was, as historian Marc Buggeln says, 'a measure of last resort for a mercilessly overheated armaments industry and in a system whose downfall was ever more likely in view of the hopeless state of the war'. When some SS managers attempted to 'modernize' their enterprises, they nevertheless took it for granted that the lives of their workers would be short and they rarely made any efforts to increase productivity by improving living conditions or food quantity. Still, memoirs of inmates of the Gross-Rosen or Neuengamme sub-camps, for example, report that conditions were far preferable to those at Auschwitz, from where many of them had been deported. Věra Hájková-Duxová, for example, says that in arriving at Christianstadt, a sub-camp of Gross-Rosen, from Auschwitz in autumn 1944, the women 'couldn't get over their amazement' when they saw proper bunks with straw mattresses. The collapse of the Third Reich in the spring of 1945 thus meant that Jewish camp inmates who were being used as slave labourers were actually (on average) in somewhat better health than those who were not. Certainly they would have died if the war had lasted longer, but ironically it was slave labour which actually prolonged the lives of many until the point at which they outlived the regime—although there are striking differences between survival rates at some sub-camps in comparison with others, as for example in the sub-camps of Neuengamme, where much depended on whether one worked inside or outdoors, or on the guards' levels of brutality. But many of these workers—Jews and non-Jews alike—were not liberated where they worked, for they had been forced to march elsewhere in the Third Reich's dying days.

The last months of the war are the most important for understanding how the state of the camps at liberation has so impacted on the world's understanding of what a concentration camp is. With the Reich collapsing, huge numbers of camp inmates were forcibly evacuated from the camps that were under imminent threat of discovery by the Allies, especially by the Red

Army, and sent into the heart of Germany on what the victims named 'death marches', a name that has subsequently become common currency since it so accurately captures the absurd viciousness of the process, and identifies the marches as part of the Holocaust. That means that the camps still in existence in early 1945 were heavily overburdened with vast numbers of already ill and dying inmates, in conditions of chaos where caring for concentration camp prisoners was low on the list of priorities for the Third Reich's administrators. Dachau in April 1945, claims historian Barbara Distel, could no longer be distinguished from the other sites of mass murder. Belsen, a camp that had been opened in 1943 as a holding camp for 'privileged' inmates (ones whom the Reich thought could be useful in negotiating with the Allies), was functioning like a death camp because huge numbers were dying there every day from lack of food and water: in March 1945 alone, 18,000 inmates died. The camp system as such was imploding along with the SS bureaucracy in general, and the individual camps were disaster zones at which immense human suffering became the norm. If there was a collapse in the distinction between the murder of the Jews and the concentration camps, it lay in the fact that the majority of Jews liberated at Dachau, Buchenwald, Sachsenhausen, and Bergen-Belsen were survivors of the camps further to the east—including many Jewish slave labourers who had been in small sub-camps—who had been marched westwards in the face of the Soviet advance.

The Nazi concentration camp system was vast and, as the Nazi empire expanded, so too did its camp network, so that it covered the whole of occupied and Axis Europe. Alongside the SS camps there were camps for POWs (including Stalags or main POW camps and Dulags or transit camps); camps for so-called *Volksdeutsche* (ethnic Germans) who were supposed to be 'resettled' in farms vacated by Poles; and forced labour camps, for example for Polish Jews in the area of occupied Poland the Nazis called the Generalgouvernement, or for *Ostarbeiter* (workers from the east) who were held in huge numbers in the Reich in terrible conditions. Such camps existed in almost every locale in Germany. The Nazis' allies also set up camps of their own, sometimes genocidal camps in their own right—as in Jasenovac in Croatia—and sometimes waystations to genocide. In Transnistria, the area of western Ukraine between the Dniester and Bug rivers occupied by the Romanians, a combination of ramshackle camps and more or less open-air dumping grounds for local and deported Jews and Roma caused immense loss of life in the first two years of the war, including the massacre of almost 48,000 Jews at Bogdanovka in December 1941.

Yet the Third Reich was a world of camps in another respect too. Just as the regime's de facto 'enemies' were eliminated through the use of concentration camps, so the *Volksgemeinschaft*, the 'people's community', was to be brought into existence and trained in martial values through the use of a variety of labour camps (*Reichsarbeitsdienstlager*) for different constituencies: Hitler Youth, BDM (Bund Deutscher Mädel or League of German Girls), and teachers, for example. Indeed, according to a law of November 1934, the term *Arbeitslager* (labour camp) was reserved for organizations which catered for *Volksgenossen* (racial comrades) and which were devoted to the honour of the German *Volk*. Camps therefore became a necessary fixture of German life, whether for those excluded from the racial community or for those who were to be drilled into it. The Labour Service camps in particular became must-see sites for foreign dignitaries and tourists alike and were regarded by Nazi commentators as 'the best means of making this National Socialist call for a *Volksgemeinschaft* a reality', as Reich Labour Leader Konstantin Hierl put it (cited in Patel).

The anti-Nazi lawyer Sebastian Haffner experienced such a camp himself when he was ordered to attend it for 'ideological training' just before taking his assessor examination in October 1933. Finding the camp and the SA men who ran it ridiculous but also threatening, Haffner and his fellow articled clerks went unenthusiastically along with what was expected of them—singing, marching, ideological instruction sessions—until he had to admit that by doing so, no matter how reluctantly, the effect was undeniable: 'By acceding to the rules of the game that was being played with us, we automatically changed, not quite into Nazis, but certainly into usable Nazi material.' Asking himself why they did go along with it, Haffner honestly admits several reasons: attending the camp had become a requirement for passing the law exams; the attendees mistrusted one another, being unable to fathom each other's real attitude towards the Nazis; and finally a 'typically German aspiration'—the 'idolization of proficiency for its own sake, the desire to do whatever you are assigned to do as well as it can possibly be done.' Besides, once the inmates were offered some proper military training, they even began to enjoy it, despite themselves. 'Thus,' Haffner writes, 'we believed we had escaped ideological training, even while we were thoroughly immersed in it.' Even more pernicious, Haffner explains that after a period in the camp, the individual began to lose a sense of himself as significant, with all thought and action in the camp being channelled in favour of the group. Waking in the night, Haffner felt ashamed to be wearing a uniform with a swastika armband—but he wore it nonetheless. He was 'in the trap of comradeship'.

Indeed, the trap of comradeship was exactly what the Nazis aimed for. It constituted the counter-image of the 'comradeship' created in the concentration camps. Where the rejected would be isolated from the rest of the society, the latter would be frogmarched into the *Volksgemeinschaft*. A society modelled on the barracks, everyday life as camp, is what the Nazis aimed at. And many celebrated it. Melita Maschmann, for example, author of a memoir of growing up in Nazi Germany, claimed that:

> Our camp community was a miniature model of what I imagined the racial community [*Volksgemeinschaft*] to be. It was a completely successful model. I have never before or after experienced so good a community, not even in places which were more homogeneous in every respect. Amongst us women there were farmers, students, workers, shop assistants, hairdressers, school pupils, office workers

and so on. The camp was led by an East Prussian farmer's daughter who had never before been outside of her own home region [*Heimat*]...Experiencing this model of the Volksgemeinschaft with such an intensive feeling of happiness produced in me an optimism which I stubbornly clung on to until 1945.

(Cited in Wildt, 'Funktionswandel', p. 80)

By contrast, even though many disliked it, like Haffner the great majority went along with it because they were afraid of the other sort of camps that awaited them if they objected. Haffner knew, when he was writing in 1939, that this variety of comradeship—the forced creation of community—could become 'the means for the most terrible dehumanization'; and he argued 'that it has become just that in the hands of the Nazis. They have drowned the Germans, who thirst after it, in this alcohol to the point of *delirium tremens*. They have made all Germans everywhere into comrades', and comradeship, Haffner pointed out, 'is part of war'. These thoughts on the use of camps for the creation of the *Volksgemeinschaft* have been confirmed by scholars, who show that there was a dialectical relationship between belonging and genocide. When Haffner wrote in 1939 that 'The general promiscuous comradeship to which the Nazis have seduced the Germans has debased this nation as nothing else could', he could not have known of the Holocaust or of the full extent of Nazi criminality more generally. But he sensed that that there was a connection between the camps for the racial comrades and the camps for the social, political, and racial rejects. The Janus-faced nature of the Nazi camps meant that a concentration camp for the eradication of enemies required few alterations to become instead a site for the education of the racially valuable members of the Volk. Inclusion and exclusion went hand in hand; the former required the latter, and vice versa.

Of course it is the 'exclusion' side of the equation for which the Third Reich's concentration camps are remembered. When the British army encountered Bergen-Belsen it was unprepared

46

for 'the world of nightmare' which it found there, as Richard Dimbleby put it in his radio despatch of 17 April 1945. Entering the camp was shocking enough, with corpses littering the site and the barely alive staggering about. But nothing prepared Dimbleby for what followed:

> I have seen many terrible sights in the last five years, but nothing, nothing approaching the dreadful interior of this hut in Belsen. The dead and the dying lay close together...They were crawling with lice and smeared with filth. They'd had no food for days, for the Germans sent it down into the camp en bloc and only those strong enough to come out of the huts could get it. The rest of them lay in the shadows getting weaker and weaker. There was no one to take the bodies away when they died and I had to look hard to see who was alive and who was dead.
>
> (Despatch reprinted in Bloxham and Flanagan (eds), *Remembering Belsen*, p. xii)

Similarly, American journalist Percy Knauth described Buchenwald on its liberation, saying that 'Until that moment, I had never fully realized what a concentration camp like Buchenwald was.' Now he felt that 'it did not seem possible that anyone who ever saw the terrible misery of Buchenwald, let alone had lived in it, would ever be able to forget it and go back to normal human living.' The scenes described by Dimbleby, Knauth, and many others in Germany in 1945 have defined how we think about concentration camps.

For many historians today, the extraordinary vileness of the Nazi camps means that it is invalid to use the term 'concentration camps' to encompass both the Nazi sites and those established by regimes in other times and places. Yet many of the first people to see the Nazi camps in 1945 made the connection explicitly, as a way of warning the world of the risk of seeing the Third Reich as a sui generis case. Knauth, for example, not only admonished his fellow Americans for failing to do anything about the Nazi camps whilst they were in existence, he went further and urged his readers to think through what the Nazi camps meant for humanity:

> And even in this year of peace and victory, we have let the concentration camp live on. We have let it live in Argentina, right in our own hemisphere. We have let it live in Egypt, where Greek soldiers who a year and a half ago revolted against a government-in-exile which had oppressed them while it held the power were clapped in prison by our British allies. We are letting it live in country after country—in Greece and in Palestine, in India and in Spain, among nations liberated and unliberated from the oppressions against which, after four long years, we were finally forced to fight. We wrote 'Four Freedoms' on our banners—freedoms for which men were dying in places we had never heard of; but now the freedoms and the places and the Buchenwalds have all receded into the unpleasant past . . . Our measure of responsibility for Buchenwald is not so great or immediate as is Germany's, but it is equal with Germany's responsibility for concentration camps as a creation of mankind. If we deny that responsibility today, as Germany did when Hitler came to power, we may find Buchenwald in our own land tomorrow.

(*Germany in Defeat*, pp. 62–3)

This kind of universalizing moralizing is not to everyone's taste. Some may find Knauth's argument that all people are to some extent responsible for things done by a certain regime unpalatable, regarding it as playing down the specific responsibility of those who created and ran the camps. Yet there are different ways we can read Knauth. He could be warning us not to regard the Nazi camps as the only manifestation of concentration camps in history. He may be reminding us that even if they are not as destructive or as synonymous with a ruling ideology as the Nazi camps, concentration camps can still exist elsewhere. And he might be telling us that bracketing off the Nazi experience—even if done for valid and justifiable reasons—might have the opposite effect to the one intended and might allow inhumanity to flourish. Indeed, it is quite clear that the camps we have encountered thus far in this book, in Cuba, the Philippines, South Africa, German South-West Africa, the Ottoman Empire, and the Third Reich, are all quite different. That it is nevertheless possible to speak of them using the same designation—concentration camps—does not mean that they are the same either empirically or morally. The existence of Dachau should not prevent us from recognizing concentration camps elsewhere. That is perhaps nowhere more clear than in the history of the Gulag, which we will examine next.

Chapter 4
The Gulag

Nikolai Averianov was 11 years old when his parents were
subjected to 'dekulakization'. In his deposition for Memorial, the
human rights organization which investigates political repression
in the USSR, he then describes the process of being deported from
the Mordovia region to the Bogatovsk region in northern Siberia.

> My father, Pyotr Averianov, was arrested at night in April, 1932, and
> taken to who knows where. Afterwards they arrested my mother,
> Varvara, in May on the night before Easter and threw us seven
> children, including me, out of the house. They sat us four older
> children on two horses, tied us up with reins so we wouldn't run
> away, and put the three smaller ones to bed with no clothing.

Along with several other families, he was locked in a railroad car
in which, after several days' travelling, people lost their minds and
starved to death. After stopping in Tomsk to pull out a few
corpses, the train carried on until it reached its final destination,
where the 'kulaks' were introduced to their 'special settlement':

> From Tomsk they took us to a pier, loaded us onto a barge, and
> we sailed up the Chulym River. I don't remember how long we
> travelled. They unloaded us onto a pier, and we walked about three
> kilometres to the village of Pesochnoe in Bogatovsk Region. Two

of the children in our family, Nastia and Vania, died on the way there. They abandoned us there, 'Live as you like!'

(Frierson and Vilensky, *Children of the Gulag*, p. 104)

By contrast with the Nazi camps, which are imprinted on the world's consciousness through images, films, testimonies, and trial records, the Gulag remains, even today, hard to imagine. 'Gulag', strictly speaking, refers to an administrative institution created in 1929, the department of the OGPU (Unified State Political Administration, replaced by the NKVD/MVD, the forerunners of the KGB) responsible for the camps: the Chief Administration of Corrective Labour Camps. For contemporaries, 'Gulag' referred solely to this authority, not to the camp system. The sites of incarceration that later came to be denominated by the name 'Gulag', thanks to Solzhenitsyn's coining of the term 'Gulag archipelago', encompassed prisons, punishment colonies, corrective labour camps, agricultural colonies, and 'special settlements'. The NKVD tended to use the terms interchangeably. As historian Felix Schnell says, these multiple forms are probably responsible for the fact that the Gulag has no ideal-typical site and to a large extent has no 'face' in the way that the Holocaust does. There was no Auschwitz in the Gulag, there are no iconic images like the *Arbeit macht frei* entrance gate, no immediately recognizable terms which take us to the heart of the matter, such as 'gas chamber'. Although some of these sites resemble Nazi camps, others, notably the special settlements, were quite different—but all were part of the Gulag (see Figure 4).

The differences between the Nazi camps and the Soviet ones are in some ways clear. Tzvetan Todorov, for example, follows David Rousset in noting the different role played by killing in the two systems:

Ironically, it was the Soviets, whose theoretical framework stressed social and historical processes, who allowed 'natural selection' to

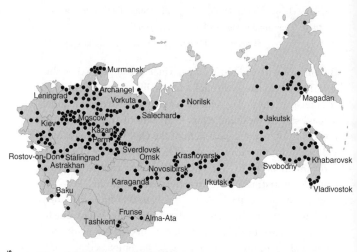

4. Map of the Gulags in the USSR.

run its course: in the gulag, hunger, cold, and sickness drove the weak to the wall. The Nazis, on the other hand, who claimed to believe in the pseudo-Darwinian doctrine of the 'survival of the fittest', used 'artificial selection' at Auschwitz and also at Ravensbrück: the SS, their doctors, and guards decided on which prisoners should die and which should be saved. The Soviets sacrificed human lives as if they were worthless, but the Nazis were overcome by a kind of 'murder madness'.

(*Hope and Memory*, p. 105)

Or, as Richard Evans reminds us, 90 per cent of inmates survived the Gulag, whereas in the Nazi camps the survival rate was less than half. The fact that in the Stalinist period between 20 per cent and 40 per cent of inmates were released every year has led historian Golfo Alexopoulos to talk of a 'revolving door' of arrest and release in the Gulag. In more philosophical vein, former resistance fighter, Buchenwald inmate, and, after the war, underground communist courier Jorge Semprun argues that 'the Russian camps are not *Marxist*, in the sense that the German camps were *Nazi*'. Hitler, says Semprun, 'put his ideas into practice, reconstructing German reality in accordance with them'. By contrast, there were different interpretations of Marxism, and many Marxist theoreticians and movements who opposed Bolshevism claimed allegiance to Marx. Rather than being Marxist, then, the Russian camps 'are *Bolshevik* camps. The Gulag is the direct, unequivocal product of Bolshevism.'

Yet in other ways, the differences seem less relevant. Margarete Buber-Neumann, a survivor of both camp systems, said that 'It is hard to know which is less humanitarian—gassing people in five minutes, or taking three months to crush them with hunger' (cited in Todorov). Besides, some of the Soviet camps have a greater claim to be thought of as 'a different planet' than do the Nazi camps, which were often in or on the edge of heavily populated towns, and which were certainly well integrated into the local economies. Inmates of Soviet prisons in or near cities were not allowed to work, because the possibility of escape was feared to be too great. But many of the camps and 'special settlements' were different: they were remote and escape was unlikely to succeed, though that did not stop people trying in large numbers. Places like Kolyma, physically isolated from the rest of the Soviet Union (until the 1970s accessible only by plane or, between April and December, by ship) and climatically shock-inducing, were much more thoroughly removed from the outside world. The mortality rate at Kolyma until 1949 was 30–40 per cent of the inmates annually; in some even more remote camps such as Chukotka or Indigirka it could reach as high as 80 per cent. The statistics are, understandably, hard to establish, with some scholars finding it hard to believe that more than half the Kolyma camp population died each year, but recent research makes the claim seem credible.

The tradition of transportation to remote regions as a form of punishment long predated the Bolshevik Revolution but the origins of the Gulag as a system of camps administered by the NKVD lies in the 1923 decision to use the Solovetski Islands in the Barents Sea as concentration camps. Two decisions taken in 1929 and 1930 were decisive for the growth of the Gulag out of the existing penal system. In June 1929, the Politburo's resolution 'On the Use of Prison Labour' allowed the OGPU to develop existing labour camps and to build new ones in mineral-rich areas. And in April 1930, the subsequent memorandum issued by Sovnarkom (Council of People's Commissars), 'On the Status of Corrective-Labour Camps', extended the repressive camp apparatus. By 1931 the OGPU was overseeing the special settlements as well as the prison camps.

The camps established on the Solovetski Islands—known as Solovki—set a dangerous precedent on the one hand and indicated the need for more thoughtful administration on the other. Described by one escapee in his 1926 account as 'an Island Hell', Solovki was in its first years a place where the prisoners were more or less abandoned, with bleak results. Under former prisoner Naftali Frenkel, the camp complex was given a more economically productive direction, thus laying the foundations for the slave labour economy in the Soviet Union. Following the Solovki debacle and the turn to Frenkel's experiments with slave labour, the Soviet authorities turned more to the idea of making the camps economically useful. Projects such as the building of the White Sea–Baltic Canal of 1931 embodied this aim. As historian Andrei Sokolov explains, the Gulag was envisaged as a 'magic wand' but, as the authorities soon discovered, they 'needed equipment, skilled labour, experienced specialists, and better working qualifications, all of which raised the cost of maintaining the Gulag'. Despite various schemes to pay workers and to bribe them with promises of reduced sentences for overfilling quotas, the Gulag was never productive. Indeed, such schemes tended to backfire as the best workers were released.

Perhaps the most notorious of the 'camps' was the Kolyma region in the Soviet Far East. Here the city of Magadan was the administrative centre of a region of nearly three million square kilometres, which reached from the Lena River to the Bering Strait, an area larger than Western Europe. Magadan's camps existed because of the area's gold reserves. Kolyma, according to Solzhenitsyn, was 'the greatest and most famous island, the pole of ferocity of that amazing country of *Gulag*'. Dal'stroi, Magadan's penal branch, was the largest entity in the labour camp system; as historian David Nordlander writes, its name, an acronym for the Far Northern Construction Trust, was 'a calculated euphemism for a ruthless organisation whose wide array of functions made it the omnipotent overlord in the Soviet northeast'.

Dal'stroi was founded in November 1931 and Stalin appointed the experienced Latvian camp director Eduard Petrovich Berzin as its head. Despite the façade of oversight by official bodies, Dal'stroi was effectively under Berzin's and Stalin's direct control. The growth in camps and the ability of the NKVD, headed by Yagoda in Moscow, to keep tight hold of the purse strings and thus of what was happening there despite the vast distance from the Kremlin, ensure that Magadan has justifiably been referred to as the 'capital of the Gulag'. Berzin's own death by shooting in August 1938 completes the Gulag script. As the 'capital of the Gulag', Magadan's operations spread over enormous distances and included some of the most infamous names of the Gulag, particularly Kolyma. The growth in prisoner numbers in Magadan mirrored the spectacular growth of the Gulag as a whole: from 9,928 in 1932 to 190,503 in September 1940.

A similar process occurred elsewhere. Vorkuta, in the Arctic north-east of Russia, became the site of one the largest camp complexes, holding about 75,000 prisoners in 1950. Coal mining began in Vorkuta in 1931 when a group of thirty-nine prisoners was sent to the uninhabited region for that purpose; it soon grew into a massive camp complex, particularly in 1937–8 as victims of the Great Terror arrived in large numbers and thus as 'political enemies' replaced 'colonists'. Although prisoners were sent there to be 'reformed', their deaths in appalling conditions meant that the reality was far grimmer than the authorities had anticipated. Ukhtpechlag camp was, according to the inspectors' own reports, 'exceptionally appalling'. By the end of 1937, Ukhtpechlag held nearly 60,000 prisoners in an area of over 700,000 square kilometres. It was split into four separate camps in May 1938. But the term 'camp' should not conjure up an image of a small, enclosed institution. One of the four camps, Vorkutlag, occupied a vast space in which the small population was not properly divided ('zonified') between prisoners and non-prisoners and in which the civilian administration was more or less indistinguishable from the camp administration. Even during the war, when control over the prisoners was tightened, not all sections of Vorkutlag had been enclosed behind barbed wire (see Figure 5).

Similar observations could be made about the other major Stalinist-era camps, such as Noril'sk or Karaganda. They covered huge areas, were divided into a number of separate penal institutions, and often there was little real distinction between the prisoner and non-prisoner zones. Yet that is not to say that the camps were not brutal; the stories and memoirs of Varlam Shalamov, Eugenia

5. Vorkuta industrial concentration camp complex, 160 km above the Arctic Circle, with Gulag camp of coal mine nos 9–10 in the foreground and coal mine 'Kapitlanya' on the horizon, 1955.

Ginzburg, Gustaw Herling, and others leave us in no doubt as to the terrible conditions in which people lived and worked, and died in huge numbers. Even when prisoners were left unescorted, a situation Shalamov depicts in his story 'Dry Rations', there was little chance of escape as these camps were so remote. 'The geography of the Archipelago was a solid obstacle to escape attempts—those endless expanses of snow or sandy desert, tundra, taiga', as Solzhenitsyn writes. Prisoners did escape from the camps but parts of the Vorkuta complex were remote enough to justify Solzhenitsyn's claim.

These remote camps and labour colonies are the ones on which our image of the Gulag has been based. They are the places of Solzhenitsyn's 'archipelago' where the guards suffered only marginally less than the prisoners and conditions were exceptionally harsh. Just getting to the camps was life-threatening; the story of Fyodor Vasilevich Mochulsky's forty-five-day trip from Moscow to Abez, where he would work as an administrator at the Sevpechlag camp, near Vorkuta, is hair-raising, involving boat journeys across the White Sea and Barents Sea, and a river boat down the Pechora River which had to be abandoned as the river unexpectedly froze, meaning the journey had to be completed on foot. Although these were not death camps, huge numbers died from overwork and starvation as the prisoners were considered expendable and easily replaceable; mass shootings occurred too on an ad hoc basis. And although there was no Auschwitz, forestry camps such as Tomasinlag have been described by historian Oleg Khlevniuk as 'provisional death camps' because of the appalling conditions and correspondingly high death rate. The case of the island camp Nazino, in the River Ob, 800 km north of Tomsk in Western Siberia, is well documented and especially cruel. Here over 10,000 'political enemies' from Moscow and Leningrad were dumped in 1933, left to fend for themselves. Nicolas Werth's description of it as *Cannibal Island* is more than apt.

Not all Soviet concentration camps were located in remote regions, however. Some of the main camps in the Western

Siberia region, for example, were located within the city limits of Tomsk and Novosibirsk. Novosibirsk's largest factory complex, Combine No. 179, was partly built with prisoner labour, as was the Chkalov Aviation Factory. In many of these cases, and indeed in some of the remote camps, the boundaries between camps and the regular population were porous. Jacques Rossi, who spent twenty-five years in Soviet camps, wrote that the Gulag was 'the most precise embodiment of the state that created it. It was not a mere slip of the tongue to say that a freed zek [inmate] had been transferred from the "small" zone to the "large" one' (cited in Ivanova). Given that the Gulag has so often been depicted as Soviet society in miniature, it is perhaps hardly surprising that the two to some extent merged into one another. Although recent popular histories of the Gulag tend to follow the Cold War script, describing it as an archipelago of isolated sites of atrocity, this is to overlook the findings of post-Cold War scholarly research. This has discovered by contrast that the term 'Gulag' covers a multiplicity of heterogeneous sites which were not all separated from the outside world. Certainly there were very isolated camps to which being sent was tantamount to a death sentence. But elsewhere, particularly in the special settlements—which were, as one historian notes, half way between freedom and the concentration camp—the situation was different and the characteristics of some of the Gulag's institutions challenge our understanding of what a concentration camp is.

Throughout the Gulag, the phenomenon of 'de-convoyed' prisoners—who were authorized to move unescorted outside the camp zone—permitted interaction between inmates and those 'outside the zone' to a surprisingly large extent. Indeed, according to historian Wilson Bell, 'in some parts of the Gulag, such as Vorkuta, it was quite common for prisoners to live outside of the [camp] zone, and the borders between camp and city frequently shifted'. These 'dezoned' prisoners (i.e. those who lived outside the zone), thanks to their living arrangements and their intermediate social and economic status, 'blurred the line between prisoners and non-prisoners'. In 1942, 2,743 prisoners in Vorkuta, nearly 10 per cent of the total, were living outside the 'zone'. Many freed inmates stayed in the area and worked in the camps as 'free' labourers, as Eugenia Ginzburg did in Magadan after her release in the late 1940s. The terminology is misleading: in fact released inmates, like the rest of the 'free' Soviet population, could not normally choose where they lived. That is why many of them, lacking alternatives, ended up working as camp administrators or guards. That is also why the city of Vorkuta, for example, exists: established as a company town in 1943, centred mainly on coal mining (in 1975, it contained the largest coal mine in Europe), its inhabitants are to a large extent descendants of former zeks and their guards; 'a strange citizenry indeed', as Alan Barenberg notes. Barenberg, the historian of Vorkuta, argues that Vorkuta is an example of a company town where 'many former prisoners successfully reintegrated themselves into Soviet society'. The same was true for the special settlers across the Soviet Union: over time, following the gradual dismantling of the special settlements after Stalin's death, the special settlers' children and grandchildren lost the sense of their parents' and grandparents' suffering and became ordinary Soviet citizens.

The reports on deconvoyed and dezoned prisoners reveal a host of fears on the part of the authorities. A 1935 report from Dmitlag bemoaned the fact that unescorted prisoners 'use the lunch break to wander round town, go to town bathhouses, make various purchases, etc. under the pretence of partaking of medical treatment or social activity in the departments of the administration of construction and the camp' (cited in Bell). Another report into several Western Siberian camps from 1952 was unimpressed by the fact that 'Several de-convoyed prisoners, taking advantage of the disorder [in the camps], freely visit population centres and drink and associate with citizens' (cited in Khlevniuk). Nevertheless, these categories of prisoners were permitted to exist because they served useful purposes; their status made them more willing to aid the regime in key industries—many were specialists in engineering, for example—and smoothed the passage between incarceration and release. At the very least, their presence indicates a lack of resources for building proper camps to house them. This situation changed in Vorkuta after 1945, when the whole camp complex was enclosed, but dezoned prisoners continued to exist, the status being granted to skilled workers as a privilege or simply as patronage, distributed at the whim of the camp directors. Former Gulag administrator Mochulsky describes the prisoners allowed to move around without an armed escort, the 'permanent railwaymen and road foremen', as ill-fed and living in difficult circumstances, especially given the harsh Arctic climate and the fact that 'these prisoner-railwaymen of the Gulag knew what kinds of punishment awaited them if there were an accident and they were blamed'. Nevertheless, he notes that 'Despite everything, they still preferred to "hang on" to this work, since it was familiar to them and it provided them the possibility of resting a little from the cruel camp regime.'

Many of the inhabitants of the city of Vorkuta, which grew up alongside the camp, were former dezoned prisoners who stayed because their labour was in demand. In the period of de-Stalinization, the geography of the camp and the city was altered so that sections of the camp from which the barbed wire had been removed simply became part of the 'outside'—the 'zone shrank' and the city expanded. Here we see how the Gulag and Soviet society at large morphed into one another. These were not 'two worlds' and as the concentrationary world shrank so it was absorbed by the outside space until the point at which the Gulag, which never ceased to exist in the Soviet Union's lifetime, became less and less relevant for the Soviet economy and more and more like a regular penitentiary system.

An important example of the merging of the 'small zone' and the 'large zone' was the black market trading and the creation of informal networks to enable survival by bypassing official channels, known as *blat*. This phenomenon might have represented a deficiency of the camp system (especially from the NKVD's point of view) but it was important for the Soviet economy, whose rigidity was otherwise stifling. The Gulag was, as Bell writes, 'an integrated part of the community, of Soviet society'. Indeed, some historians argue that even the distinction between 'small' and 'large' zones does not capture the extent to which the Gulag was inseparable from Soviet society. Russian historian Galina Ivanova, for example, argues that 'The territory of the "small zone" essentially coincided with the territory of the Soviet Union.' If that was the case then clearly a variety of interactions could occur that would have been unthinkable in the case of Nazi camps. The latter were very much part of local economies and brought all manner of economic, sexual, and social opportunities for locals and guards alike; but opportunities for inmates to have contact with outsiders were severely limited.

Just as we are now better informed about the development of the Nazi camps over time, so it is necessary to distinguish different phases of deportation to the Gulag corresponding to different phases of Stalinist terror. The deportations of 1929–30 coincided with the 'dekulakization' programme and filled the camps with farmers and peasants. In 1930–1, of the two million peasants deported, more than half a million were dead, had escaped, or had disappeared. The Great Terror of 1937–8—which remains largely and incorrectly synonymous with the Gulag in the popular imagination—destroyed the careers and lives of huge numbers of communists, as the paranoid dynamic of unmasking 'plots' and 'bourgeois wreckers' brought fear and terror to the heart of the Communist Party. As many as 1.6 million 'enemies of the people' or 'counter-revolutionaries' were arrested in that period, though few had actually done anything to justify the accusations—and their spouses and children, also deported in huge numbers, certainly had not. The last potential sites of opposition to Stalin were eliminated but in the process the Soviet Union's military and economic experts were also decimated.

Before the war, a new phase of deportations occurred as Moscow's paranoia extended to national groups. In 1935, Poles, Finns, and Balts were deported from the Soviet Union's 'sensitive' western borders to Kazakhstan, Tajikistan, or Siberia. In 1937, 'suspect' peoples who inhabited Soviet border regions or areas of Eastern Europe occupied by the Soviets were deported: Finns, Poles, Romanians, Ukrainians, Balts, Koreans, Iranians, and others, all victims of Soviet paranoia about enemies within. The whole population of Soviet Koreans—172,000 people—was deported to Kazakhstan or Uzbekistan on suspicion of collaborating with the Japanese, a claim which under normal circumstances would rightly have been dismissed as absurd. The war, of course, did nothing to quell this paranoia. The Volga Germans were deported in 1941; half a million Chechens and Ingush were deported in 1943–4 as 'Nazi collaborators', as were Kalmyks, Karachays, Balkars, and Crimean Tatars. The Volga Germans, like the Crimean Tatars, were never permitted to return home. Finally, later in 1944, border communities around the Black Sea, including Bulgars, Greeks, and Armenians, were deported, as were Turks and Kurds along the border with Turkey and Iran.

Many of these groups of people—up to 50 per cent of whom were children—were dumped in inhospitable areas of Siberia or Kazakhstan and left to fend for themselves; others were sent to existing camps and settlements. Whole communities were devastated, as this testimony concerning Chechen suffering indicates:

> Adzhigulsum Adzhimambetova's husband had been seized by the fascists. She was left with three children, one girl and two boys. Her family starved just as ours did. No one gave them either material or moral support. As a result the daughter died of starvation to begin with, and then the two sons, both on the same day. The mother was so weak with hunger she could not move. Then the owner of the house threw the two little infant corpses out onto the street, on the edge of an irrigation canal. Some Crimean Tatar children dug little

graves and buried little ones. How can I speak of this? I can hardly even bear to remember it.

(Frierson and Vilensky, Children of the Gulag, p. 294)

Wartime conditions in the already crowded camps were appalling and new deportees suffered greatly. The period of the war and not that of the Great Terror was the most deadly for the Gulag's inhabitants: in 1942 and 1943 about a fifth of all inmates died: more than 400,000 people. This fact once again indicates how the Gulag mirrored conditions in Soviet society in general: the war brought immense hardship to Soviet citizens, who were killed in far greater numbers than anywhere else in Europe. Their suffering was unimaginable to Americans, for whom the war never reached their shores after Pearl Harbor. Coercive labour measures were especially severe in the Soviet Union as factories were evacuated to the east, women and young workers replaced men, and hours worked were exceptionally long, with the reward being food and clothing rationing, highly restrictive living conditions, and stringent punishments for infractions in order to enforce labour discipline. If the number of Gulag inmates had halved by 1944, that was because one million were released to work in war-related industries and some two million died on the front, many as members of so-called 'penal battalions', that is to say, as cannon fodder. The focus of the camps themselves was on their economic usefulness to the war effort in a way that greatly exceeded previous efforts to extract use-value from the inmates. Many members of the 'punished peoples' were used in this way, as were some four million POWs, who were forced to work in a 'special contingent' (*speckontingent*). The distinction between Gulag inhabitants and 'free' labourers was, as Schnell notes, blurred more during the war than at any other time previously.

After the war the Gulag grew again. Returning Soviet POWs who had survived the murderous captivity of German camps—some three million died in gruesome conditions—were immediately deported to 'verification' and 'filtration' camps, from where they were usually either sent into exile or returned into society after a few months. Hundreds of thousands of people were deported from lands reconquered from the Nazis or newly incorporated into the Soviet Union: the Baltic States, Western Ukraine, Bessarabia, Western Belarus. By 1950 there were some 2.8 million camp inmates and in 1953, when Stalin died, still at least 2.5 million, some 11 per cent of whom were working without guards. The late 1940s/early 1950s were thus the years when the Gulag reached its greatest size. Yet economically speaking the Gulag was unprofitable and labour productivity reached a mere 50–60 per cent of civilian equivalents. Beria released 1.5 million inmates three weeks after Stalin's death, using the opportunity to put into place a long-held MVD aim to cut the Gulag's costs by removing from its purview petty criminals and recidivists and to make the camp system less of a drain on the economy. Yet the Gulag as such was not dismantled, even after Khrushchev's 'secret speech' denouncing Stalin's crimes in 1956; in fact, although the department called 'Gulag' was closed down in 1957, the camp system existed until the end of the USSR itself.

Yet it did change. Hundreds of thousands of inmates were released, especially 'politicals' and members of 'punished peoples'. Some received full rehabilitation. Yet the Gulag carried on incarcerating people, though after 1956 they generally knew why they had been arrested. Apart from common criminals, political and religious dissidents were at most risk. When Avraham Shifrin published his *First Guidebook to Prisons and Concentration Camps of the Soviet Union* in 1980, the book, presented like a regular tourist guide, included a section on 'extermination camps'. What this meant was not Treblinka-like facilities, but places where prisoners were forced to work with dangerous machines such that they 'face a virtually certain death'. Despite the Cold War tone, the book documents the still vast extent of the prison network, especially the cruel use of psychiatric prisons for people who protested against Soviet policies or demanded the right to leave the country. Only after Mikhail Gorbachev came to power in 1985 and initiated the policy of *glasnost* was it possible to begin to speak openly about the Gulag, although the decades of silence were not easily broken and many have remained afraid to speak even since the demise of Soviet communism.

The Soviet leadership continued to believe in its rhetoric of 're-education' until the end. 'You have been brought here to enable you to reform yourselves—to realise your crimes, and to prove by honest, self-sacrificing work that you are loyal to socialism and to our beloved Stalin. Hurrah, Comrades!', as Vladimir Petrov and his fellow deportees were greeted on their arrival in Kolyma. Solzhenitsyn regarded such slogans as mockery and many prisoners certainly felt the same, but it is not clear that they were in fact meant as such. In the early 1930s the Soviets published books and newspapers celebrating 'socialist labour' inside the camps and special settlements, just as they did outside them and abroad in various languages. So too did the Nazis, with articles in the German press showing how Dachau was reforming its degenerate inmates. The difference was that after such publications were banned for the general Soviet public in the late 1930s, the Soviets continued to celebrate forced labour as a way of 're-forging' the prisoner in camp newspapers inside the camps themselves. Articles celebrating Stakhanovism amongst the workers and socialist construction were common. As historian Steven Barnes says, the Soviets chose—they certainly had the means—not to create a 'truly genocidal institution' in the Gulag. Although mortality rates were high, the camps were used for forced labour to keep the economy going in a way—albeit highly unproductive—that the Nazi camps did not, at least until the crisis of the Third Reich's war led to the Nazis' reluctant decision to use camp labour. The Gulag spanned the length of the Soviet Union and lasted as long as the USSR did because transportation to remote regions was, as human geographer Judith Pallot notes, both a process of 'regulation by exclusion' and 'a means of delivering labour to places where it was needed'. And if administrators like Mochulsky started to question the value of the Gulag later on in life, speaking of 'the monstrous inventions of the Stalinist regime', at the time of his service (1940–6) there is no doubt that he accepted the need for the railway being built between Kotlas and Vorkuta and the wisdom of using 'fascists' and 'criminals' to do so.

Remarkably, some survivors even look back on their years in the Gulag with something approaching nostalgia or pride. Sira Stepanovna Balashina, for example, came from a family deported as kulaks in 1930 from Kurgan *oblast* (region) in south-western Siberia to Perm *oblast* in the Urals. Both her parents and her sister died in the famine of 1932–3 and Sira alone remained, spending her life working in the forest. When interviewed about her experiences at the age of 92 in 2004, Balashina recalled that she worked hard and well, and as a consequence was rewarded with the Medal for Valiant Labour during the war and, when she retired, the Medal for a Veteran of Labour. Despite being officially freed from forced labour shortly after the war, Balashina remained in Perm and continued to work in the forest. As her interviewers, Gheith and Jolluck, note, the medals 'confirmed her identity as a contributing Soviet citizen. Balashina's pride in her medals shows that rather than reject the values of the system that had repressed her, she internalised them.' One historian found that of the children of deportees she interviewed, 'only a few expressed strong anti-Soviet attitudes regarding the repression or destruction of their parents' lives'. Some even became party members and played an active role in public life. Perhaps when one considers that children being brought up in the Gulag played games such as 'searching for and uncovering enemies' or 'hot pursuit', this attitude becomes more comprehensible. The fact is, though, that many of the former special settlers became what historian Kate Brown calls the Soviet Union's 'hereditary underclass', who were never able to get rid of the feeling that they were second-class citizens.

Prisoners in the Gulag could survive for many years, if circumstances permitted it; there was life in the Gulag. Furthermore, there was a constant stream of prisoners being released, showing that 'redeemability, at least for some segment of the prisoner population, was never totally abandoned' (Barnes). German political prisoners did sometimes survive twelve years—the duration of the Third Reich—in the Nazi camps, but these were very few in number. In the Gulag, the border between camp and the 'large' zone was not fixed and the phenomenon of de-convoyed prisoners has no equal in the Nazi case. If Dachau epitomizes the concentration camp, then many of the Gulag's sites of incarceration other than the prisons and corrective labour camps do not exactly meet the criteria. Historian Nicolas Werth writes that the Gulag was 'a world where administrative chaos, sloppiness, indifference, chance and neglect seem to have played a more important role than any systematic intention to exterminate'. In other words, Arendt seems to be right: the Soviet camps represent purgatory where the Nazi ones represent hell.

And yet, there is another way of seeing this issue. In terms of numbers, far more people suffered in the Gulag than in the Nazi camps: an average of 2.5 million annually, with a peak of 2.8 million in 1950, meaning somewhere in the region of 20 million Soviet citizens passed through the camps between 1928 and 1953, about one-third political prisoners and 10–15 per cent criminal recidivists. At least 1.6 million people died in the Gulag and probably more than one million died during transportation. More important, particularly during the Stalinist period, the difference between inside and outside the camps was one of degree; according to Nordlander, 'events behind the barbed wire in many respects encapsulated the key realities of Stalinism'. Most ordinary workers endured appalling working conditions, poor standards of housing and food, and the constant threat of hunger, terror, and punishment. Under collectivization, peasants and farmers were not free to move where they chose until the 1970s and in many cases 'the peasants' living standard was no different or

even lower than the living standard of the deported "kulaks"'
(Khlevniuk). The Gulag 'mirrored the day-to-day functioning of
Soviet society', as Bell puts it. As Andrey Vyshinski, the main
prosecutor of the Great Terror trials, explained, 'All Soviet penal
policy is based on a dialectical combination of the principle of
repression and compulsion with the principle of persuasion
and re-education... The two-in-one-task is suppression plus
re-education of anyone who can be re-educated' (cited in Barnes).
This applied to Soviet society in general, not just the Gulag,
and the recent focus of historians on the permeability of the
Gulag should be not be understood as downplaying the
phenomenon but as indicating the extent to which the Soviet
Union as a whole was brutalized. Where the Nazis sought to
model the *Volksgemeinschaft* on the barracks, the Soviets
dreamed of society as repressive factory.

With searing honesty, Gustaw Herling recalls his 'horror and
shame of a Europe divided into two parts by the line of the Bug,
on one side of which millions of Soviet slaves prayed for liberation
by the armies of Hitler, and on the other millions of victims of
German concentration camps awaited deliverance by the Red
Army as their last hope'. Yet there was a crucial difference between
the Nazi camps and the Gulag: what we now call the Holocaust.
The death camp broke with human experience in a way that the
Gulag, however brutal, did not. Recent scholarship on the
Holocaust has tended to turn our focus away from the death
camps, reminding us (quite rightly) that nearly half of the
six million Jewish victims were killed by face-to-face shooting in
pits in Eastern Europe or were starved to death in the ghettos.
Auschwitz only became fully operational when the Holocaust was
at its end, when the Jews of Hungary were deported in spring
1944: the images we recognize from Birkenau are from this
period. Nevertheless, there is a reason why Auschwitz has
become the symbol of the Holocaust and of the capacity for evil
in general: it is the clearest instantiation of the intent to kill that
human beings have yet devised.

Chapter 5
The wide world of camps

A percentage of the continent's population had become quite accustomed to the thought that they were outcasts. They could be divided into two main categories: people doomed by biological accident of their race and people doomed for their metaphysical creed or rational conviction regarding the best way to organise human welfare.

As Arthur Koestler's words from his novel *Scum of the Earth* (1941) make plain, the Third Reich's and Soviet Union's camps were not the only ones to exist before and during the Second World War. Japanese camps for Allied soldiers and civilians during the Pacific War, the Croatian camp at Jasenovac, the French internment camps in the south of France, Italy's island and African camps, and the Romanian occupation of Transnistria, which essentially became a giant, open-air concentration camp, all suggest that the Nazis' allies were willing users of camps, some more brutal and destructive than others. The democratic countries have also been accused of making use of concentration camps; the charge might have some validity, although here we can see degrees of difference between the Nazi/Soviet camps and the British/American. In the case of the British, one sometimes hears that internment camps for 'enemy aliens' or, after the war, the use of internment camps on Cyprus to hold Jewish DPs—Holocaust survivors making the 'illegal' journey to Palestine—were concentration camps. In the

American case, the wartime decision to intern American citizens of Japanese descent is often discussed using this vocabulary, with books with titles such as *Concentration Camps USA* being quite common. Were these institutions concentration camps?

After the war, concentration camps rapidly came to appear synonymous with the Third Reich. Yet as we have seen, concentration camps were by no means the invention of the Nazis, nor—if we exclude the death camps—were the Nazis' camps necessarily more deadly or brutal than those of other regimes. The Third Reich's characteristics as a whole—Nazism as a political ideology, the 'racial community' as an aspiration, the dreams of a German-dominated, racially reordered European empire—were the factors that made Nazism so apocalyptically destructive: the inseparability of word and deed in Nazism. Although the camp system was central to the Nazis' plans, especially for the creation of a helot population of Slavs who would serve their racial masters, when we consider them purely as institutions in their own right it is hard to say that the Nazi concentration camps were very different from those elsewhere. In fact, we can see that the Nazi camps provided the inspiration for camps in other countries after 1945, as in Argentina and Chile, or communist prison camps such as Piteşti in Romania. Some of the Nazi camps even continued to be used as camps for political prisoners, what the Soviets in their occupation zone of Germany called 'special camps'.

It is unsurprising, then, that shortly after the war the continued existence of camps in the world was a cause of grave concern to certain groups of intellectuals. In 1950, for example, the newly founded Commission internationale contre le régime concentrationnaire (CICRC) undertook investigations into camps in post-Civil War Spain. It was supported in the endeavour by the Buchenwald survivor and (at least in France) well-known author David Rousset. Rousset had coined the term *L'Univers concentrationnaire* in his book of that title in 1946 and now, as a co-founder of the Rassemblement démocratique révolutionnaire, an anti-Stalinist party of the left, he was keen to rebut accusations from communists that the CICRC's focus was only on the Soviet Union, as it had been in its first inquiry. It would also go on to investigate the use of camps in Greece, China, Tunisia, and Algeria.

Taking the Nazi camps as its point of departure—because here 'each of its characteristics were pushed to the extreme'—the CICRC set out that its aim was to determine

> if there exists or not, in the countries under consideration, a
> concentrationary regime or concentrationary characteristics, such a
> regime being defined by the arbitrary deprivation of liberty,
> inhumane detention conditions, the exploitation of detainees'
> labour for the benefit of the state.

The CICRC was aware of the double risk: that one might consider acceptable anything which didn't reach the degree of severity of the Nazi camps on the one hand or that one might decide to call a 'concentration camp' anything which one might find unacceptable on the other. Those problems have dogged comparative studies of concentration camps and fascist or totalitarian societies ever since.

That is hardly surprising when one considers the numerous different sorts of camp settings that have existed since the war: internment camps, refugee camps, detention centres, and so on. In examining some of them now, I want to keep open the question as to whether they should all be called concentration camps. Most will probably agree that the term is not applicable in some cases. Yet all the examples I discuss below are of camps where civilians were held against their will—to a greater or lesser extent.

Italy, France, and Spain

In Italy islands such as Lipari, Pantelleria, and Lampedusa south of Sicily and two of the Tremiti Islands in the southern Adriatic were used to confine political enemies. The practice of internal exile for political outcasts had existed in Italy since the 19th century but was expanded under Mussolini. Whilst the Fascist regime made much of the comfort in which a few former parliamentarians lived in their island prisons, especially on Lipari, the reality for most political detainees was quite different. These colonies, in which political detainees often lived alongside common criminals, 'soon came to resemble true internment camps, with most detainees living in common barracks', as historian Michael Ebner puts it. When the regime also started expelling the 'least dangerous' detainees to villages in the south after 1935 and then started to use the labour of detainees for land reclamation projects, it was presiding over what Ebner calls a 'Fascist archipelago' which formed just part of the regime's way of imposing its discipline on the Italian population. Within it, the tiny islands of Ventotene and San Nicola were especially well suited to confinement, with few natural resources and high cliffs. The latter, says Ebner, 'resembled a true concentration camp', since there was nothing there but a castle whose row houses served as barracks. Furthermore, the detainees were subjected to continual surveillance and controls on their ability to meet or move about freely. They were not held in these places in order to die, but 'the experience killed many of them and left many others gravely and chronically ill'.

But Italian camps were not found only on small islands off the coast of Italy; nor were they used solely to confine Italian political enemies. The historian Luigi Reale says that fifty-two 'fascist concentration camps', holding about 10,000 civilians, were set up all over Italy between 1940 and 1943, 'directly influenced by Mussolini's race laws that he introduced in 1938'—that is, primarily for Jews and Gypsies, but also foreign citizens. These were often buildings such as castles, former convents, or prisons that were adapted for use as camps, although at Marconia (Pisticci) and Ferramonti (Tarsia), the latter of which was established to hold Italian and non-Italian Jews, there were purpose-built camps surrounded by barbed wire. Internment in these camps was often deadly, as Tone Ferenc, a Slovenian eye-witness, reported:

The camp was surrounded by barbed wire, but there was a small
passage through to get to the administration that was in the school
on top of the hill. Down below I saw a huge crowd of women and
children. Cries would go up to curdle the blood. The little ones used
to cry. They were half naked, with emaciated faces and their bellies
distended from hunger; their eyes were glazed over in desperation
because of their privations. Men would be sitting on the ground,
dropping from fatigue. They would try to pick the fleas off
themselves.

(cited in Reale, *Mussolini's Concentration Camps*, p. 114)

The most notorious Italian camp was the Risiera (rice-processing
factory) di San Sabba, near Trieste, where some 5,000 were killed
in Italy's only death camp, and a further 20,000 were deported
to Auschwitz and other Nazi camps. It was established during
the violent last stage of the war as the main camp in the
German-designated region of Adriatisches Küstenland
(Adriatic Coast).

Italian camps were not found solely in Italy itself; in Albania,
Somalia, Libya, and Slovenia, the Italians also set up camps.
Between 1930 and 1933, some 40,000 camp inmates died from
hunger, illness, and overwork. There are even indications of an
attempt to create in 1932 an 'extermination camp' for Italian
political prisoners in the Libyan Sahara, in Gasr Bu Hadi, 478 km
south-east of Tripoli. In the end financial constraints meant it was
not built but the idea shows the logic of fascism's radical exclusion
taken to its extreme.

This logic is visible in the French camps set up to house exiles
from Spain and the Francoist camps created during and after the
Civil War. Republican exiles who had been interned in France had
already experienced what would later become hallmarks of the
fascist camps: brutal treatment behind barbed wire, exposure to
the elements, the torment of being so close to people outside living
normal lives. Some of these camps, especially the beach

6. 'What about Us, Mr Macmillan?', David Low cartoon, *Evening Standard*, 26 February 1943.

internment camps of Argelès, St Cyprien, and Le Barcarès, were built at short notice to house refugees. Others, like Le Vernet, where Koestler was interned, or Gurs, where Hannah Arendt was held, were consciously established by the French authorities as punishment camps. From them, the French deported—to almost certain death—several thousand to Gestapo control or to brutal work camps in North Africa (see Figure 6). Koestler is quick to point out that Le Vernet was not Dachau:

In Liberal-Centigrade, Vernet was the zero-point of infamy; measured in Dachau-Fahrenheit it was still 32 degrees above zero. In Vernet beating-up was a daily occurrence; in Dachau it was prolonged until death ensued. In Vernet people were killed for lack of medical attention; in Dachau they were killed on purpose. In Vernet half of the prisoners had to sleep without blankets in

20 degrees of frost; in Dachau they were put in irons and exposed
to the frost.

(Scum of the Earth, p. 94)

Yet as historian Helen Graham notes, 'in the very possibility of
comparison, Koestler reminds us that here in the network of
internment and "punishment camps" for brigaders and refugees
that covered the landscape of Roussillon in "peace time", the
European concentration camp universe was already in existence'.
Those held in Le Vernet, Gurs, or one of the other small
French camps were 'excluded from all "nations" and thus
devoid of both the symbolic value and rights such
membership afforded'.

The camps in Spain were entirely premised on the need for
discipline and punishment; Franco's carceral universe was
co-extensive with Spain. Following his victory in the Civil War,
Franco set out to ensure that those he deemed the 'anti-Spain'
would be punished for their support for the Republic. At least
60,000 people—the figure is the regime's own—were held without
any judicial involvement in 1940 alone. A vast expansion of the
prison universe took place so that buildings from schools to
warehouses were pressed into service; at the same time, 'a
constellation of labour battalions, work brigades and other
instruments of slave labour such as military penal colonies'
stretched across Spain. Violence, as the leading historian of the
Spanish camps, Javier Rodrigo, notes, was 'the rock upon which
the Franco regime was built'. The CICRC noted in its 1953 report
that, as in a concentration camp regime, 'inmates suffered dire
material conditions and extreme forms of arbitrary violence that
frequently led to their deaths'. They were also subjected to forced
labour, whether still imprisoned or whether 'released' in order
to join labour battalions or under the scheme known chillingly
as 'Punishment Redemption through Work' (Redención de
Penas por el Trabajo), battalions 'that depended directly on the
concentration camp structure'.

According to Rodrigo, more than half a million Spaniards and other Europeans passed through the more than 180 camps which made up the Francoist concentration camp system. The largest, Miranda de Ebro, opened in November 1936 and remained in existence until 1947 (others lasted considerably longer). As of June 1937, they were administered by the Prisoner Concentration Camps Inspectorate (Inspección de Campos de Concentración), which, as Rodrigo notes, 'is eerily reminiscent of Eicke's Nazi Inspectorate of 1934'. Indeed, in 1940 Himmler inspected Franco's camps and prisons and Spanish officials visited Sachsenhausen. Yet until recently Franco's camp system had been largely forgotten, perhaps because it was not exposed and defeated in war, meaning that the regime's longevity allowed it to align itself with the Cold War West. The irony, as Helen Graham notes, is that 'a Western order that retrospectively mythologized its opposition to Nazism as opposition to the camp universe, and which denounced this too as the ultimate offence of Stalinism, patronized a regime in Spain that was, like the Soviet Union's, based on mass murder and its own gulag'.

Liberal internment

By comparison with the Italian or Spanish examples, which followed the radicalizing logic of fascism, the internment of civilians by the liberal democracies was quite different. Yet the American decision to intern Japanese Americans and the British decision to intern German Jewish 'enemy aliens' have received considerable criticism, not least because their sites of internment are often described as concentration camps.

Following the bombing of Pearl Harbor, Japanese Americans came under suspicion. In the anti-Japanese clamour, this statement from leading anti-Japanese campaigner Lieutenant-Colonel John L. De Witt was typical:

> I have little confidence that the enemy aliens are law-abiding or loyal in any sense of the word. Some of them yes; many, no,

particularly the Japanese. I have no confidence in their loyalty whatsoever. I am speaking now of the native born Japanese—117,000—and 42,000 in California alone.

Ultimately it was President Roosevelt's decision to intern the Japanese, one he took on the basis of his own personal antipathy and because anti-Japanese feeling was generally strong—historian Roger Daniels puts it down to 'the general racist character of American society', as illustrated in the Dr Seuss cartoon (see Figure 7). Indeed, the decision to intern the Japanese Americans was made before Pearl Harbor.

In May 1942 Miné Okubo and her brother were incarcerated, along with thousands of others, in Tanforan Assembly Center, a race track in San Bruno near San Francisco. A young woman

7. 'Waiting for the Signal from Home', Dr Seuss cartoon, *PM*, 13 February 1942.

who had studied in Europe, Okubo produced a record of her internment which combines comic-style line drawings with wry comments. She records, for example, that letters from friends in Europe 'told me how lucky I was to be free and safe at home'. The camp was still being built when she arrived and Okubo's description of the barracks, the latrines, and wash halls seems familiar to us from descriptions of earlier camps:

> We were close to freedom and yet far from it. The San Bruno streetcar line bordered on the camp on the east and the main state highway on the south. Streams of cars passed by all day. Guard towers and barbed wire surrounded the entire center. Guards were on duty day and night.

Yet the presence of a post office, laundry buildings, a library, and schools, and the fact that internees could receive guests, clearly indicate that Tanforan was no Dachau. Nevertheless, the Japanese Americans were being held against their will without having committed a crime, and were being kept under watch in guarded, fenced-in camps. This fact leaves some historians, such as Tetsuden Kashima, in no doubt as to what to call them:

> The most accurate overall descriptive term is concentration camp—that is, a barbed-wire enclosure where people are interned or incarcerated under armed guard. Some readers might object to the use of this term, believing that it more properly applies to the Nazi camps of World War II. Those European camps were more than just places of confinement, however; many were established to provide slave labor for the Nazi regime or to conduct mass executions. I contend that such camps are more properly called Nazi slave camps or Nazi death camps.
>
> (*Judgment without Trial*, p. 8)

Even if one rejects the claim that Tanforan, Minidoka, Manzanar, and the other incarceration sites should be described as concentration camps, calling them 'internment camps' or 'assembly centres' should not make us think that the experience was somehow pleasant or that the decision to intern Japanese Americans was a credit to a democratic state. All that really happened was that, as Roger Daniels puts it, 'The myth of military necessity was used as a fig leaf for a particular variant of American racism.' Indeed, the practice set a precedent for post-war America: at the height of the Cold War the Emergency Detention Act (1950) gave the president the right to set up camps for 'The detention of persons who there is reasonable grounds to believe will commit or conspire to commit espionage or sabotage' (Sec. 101 [14]). Daniels observed in 1971 that 'Any foreseeable use of these concentration camps will be for ideological rather than racial enemies of the republic.' Although the act was partially repealed by the 1971 Non-Detention Act, Daniels here presciently foresaw Guantánamo Bay.

The internment of Japanese Americans was by no means the only example of a supposedly democratic country succumbing to fears of enemies within and incarcerating innocent people. The Americans interned Germans too. In Britain, German and Austrian Jews and Italians were absurdly targeted at the outbreak of war as a potential fifth column—as good an illustration of the power of populist paranoia as any in history. The result was that some 27,000 were interned, in a number of sites including Seaton in Devon or at Huyton near Liverpool, but the majority on the Isle of Man, where civilians had been interned during the First World War too. Several thousand of them were deported to Canada. As François Lafitte, author of a still relevant, powerful study of the policy reflected, internment was the result of panic and prejudice among government ministers and unchecked rumour-mongering by the popular press. Lafitte also observed that

> Both in the Press and in public speeches certain gentlemen
> whose pro-Nazi views were notorious in peacetime were among
> the loudest in the clamour to 'intern the lot'. Protestations of
> super-patriotism in this cheap and easy form have often been the

rather obvious defence-mechanism resorted to by men about whose patriotism there was some doubt.

The policy was stupid and cruel, and the conditions in which the internees lived were hardly pleasant. Yet in this case one cannot speak of a concentration camp; the exiles' self-designation as 'His Majesty's Most Loyal Enemy Aliens' hardly suggests people who were at bitter odds with their captors. Indeed, one internee wrote that

> the most interesting point in the internment problem is not how much the interned have had to suffer—for suffering is general all over the world at present—but how far they have been able to stand up, spiritually, to their trial, and to transform their adversities into productive experience (cited in Seyfert).

Nevertheless, even if one cannot speak of British concentration camps, it was the case, as Lafitte pointed out, that internment represented 'an authoritarian trend ... in our home life', suggesting that the spread of illiberal ideas concerning foreigners, citizenship, and national belonging was very hard for the democracies to resist when the fascist countries seemed to be in the ascendant.

The ambiguity of liberal incarceration was particularly apparent in the DP camps that were set up in Germany and Austria after the war. Immediately on war's end there were some seven million DPs in occupied Germany; by September 1945 in a remarkable feat of logistics given the war-torn state of Central Europe, some six million of them had been helped to return to their homes. The last million were the so-called 'hard-core' cases, mostly Poles and Ukrainians—some with questionable wartime records—who refused to return to countries being taken over by communist regimes. There was also a contingent of approximately 100,000 Eastern European Jews, survivors of the Holocaust, who had no homes to go back to, whose communities no longer existed, whose families had been murdered, and whose property had been stolen. In 1946 they were joined by Jews, including complete family units, returning to Europe after spending the war in exile in the Soviet Union, mostly in Central Asia. Many thousands had lost their lives there but this exile also facilitated the survival of tens of thousands of Jews who would surely have been murdered by the Nazis had they remained in situ and not fled or been deported by the Soviets in 1940–1. So by the end of 1946, there were some 250,000 Jewish DPs in camps in Germany and, to a much lesser extent, in Austria and Italy.

These camps were there because the Jewish DPs, assuming that after the war their suffering would elicit support from those who had liberated them, demanded access to the US and Palestine. These, unfortunately, were the two places to which they were least likely to be granted access. Many survivors found their way to Britain, Australia, and Latin America, but to Palestine only in large numbers after the Israeli declaration of independence in May 1948 (the *brichah* scheme for illegal immigration had helped many already) and to the US after the amendment of the DP Act in 1950, when the numbers were much reduced in any case. In the years in between, the relations between the DPs and the British and American authorities soured, and the DPs themselves made great play of the fact that they were being held in an Allied version of Nazi concentration camps. This made for powerful Zionist propaganda and gave the Soviets the opportunity to attack British imperialism in the context of the emerging Cold War. The problem was exacerbated by American criticism of the camps; Earl Harrison, in his summer 1945 report on the DP camps, wrote that 'we appear to be treating the Jews as the Nazis treated them except that we do not exterminate them'. The Anglo-American Committee of Inquiry on Palestine concurred in spring 1946 and restated Harrison's demand that 100,000 Jewish DPs should be immediately permitted to enter Palestine. In the meantime children marched in the DP camps—such as Zeilsheim or Belsen—demanding the free world to recognize their continued 'imprisonment', and anti-British campaigners used slogans such as 'British floating Dachau' to describe *brichah* ships seized by the British or chanted 'Down with Bevin, the successor to Hitler.'

Even more than the DP camps in Germany, which at least could justifiably be represented as emergency housing for desperate people, the British camps on Cyprus for illegal immigrants to Palestine were open to the charge of being 'concentration camps'. For here, the Jews who arrived were not simply being housed where they had been liberated or where they had found themselves after discovering the loss of their homes; they were rather being intercepted and prevented from exercising their will. The result was disastrous for Britain's moral standing in the world. 'Standing on this sun-baked forlorn island,' wrote Ira Hirschmann, the personal representative of Fiorello La Guardia, head of the United Nations Relief and Rehabilitation Administration (UNRRA), whilst waiting for a plane in Cyprus in May 1946,

> how could one imagine, even in his most sinister dreams, that within the next few months it would become the prison of more than 30,000 Jewish refugees, seized by His Majesty's Royal Navy, taken from tiny, leaking ships bound for Palestine, and that the British government would so soon take over Hitler's role as keeper of the concentration camps, and immortalize Cyprus along with names like Dachau, Belsen and Maidanek?

Such statements were hyperbolic, designed to achieve a political goal; but even if no one was being tortured or starved to death in the Cyprus DP camps, their presence so close to Palestine indicated British weakness rather than strength. It seemed as if it were only a matter of time before the British would yield to the DPs' demands and the clear continuity in the DPs' experience of incarceration was deeply embarrassing for the British, who were rightly celebrated as having helped to save many thousands of survivors in the preceding years.

The post-war DP camps were not concentration camps because those in them were not without legal or other forms of representation. Had they not been holding out to go to particular places, the non-Jews could have returned 'home' any time they liked—although for those going back to places like Ukraine or the Baltic States, which were being incorporated into the Soviet Union, this was tantamount to suicide. The Jews were more at the will of the authorities since they had nowhere to return to. Yet once again it is the imagery of camps that is so shocking rather than the actual continuity in experience that mattered—the British- and American-run DP camps were very far from being concentration camps in the sense that is usually understood: they were thriving communities with schools, kindergartens, presses, religious institutions, vocational training schools, sporting associations, and political movements. Even so, the people in them wanted nothing more than to leave for somewhere of their own choosing. The camps in Cyprus have a greater claim to be called concentration camps, not least because the colonial setting suggests a kind of population management that echoes previous episodes. Yet again, the camps themselves functioned like enclosed societies—though there were contacts with the local population too—and although the fact of being held in camps made for good propaganda, the DPs' claims that they were being held in the British version of Dachau does not stand up to scrutiny.

These fundamental distinctions between Nazi camps and DP camps cannot be applied in the case of the 'special camps' in the Soviet occupation zone of Germany. Following long-term Allied plans as definitively set out in the Potsdam Agreement of 2 August 1945, the Soviets (like the British and Americans) arrested and interned Nazi functionaries in ten 'special camps' at the end of the war. These camps remained in existence until 1950; among them were Sachsenhausen (Special Camp No. 2) and Buchenwald (Special Camp No. 7), the latter of which, though liberated by the Americans, fell into the Soviets' occupation zone and was therefore administered by the Soviets as of August 1945. According to figures released by the

Soviets to the GDR's CDU interior minister, Peter-Michael Diestel, in 1990, there were 122,671 Germans imprisoned in the special camps. Of these, 42,889 died whilst in the camp and a further 756 were sentenced to death and executed. In other words, although the absolute figures for internment were similar to those in the American and British zones, the rate of death in the camps (35 per cent) was far higher in the Soviet camps even though conditions in some of the American and British administered ones were far from adequate. In 1984, when the mass graves of somewhere between 6,000 and 13,000 inmates were discovered in Buchenwald, the communist authorities decided not to mention the fact in the new exhibition which opened in the former camp the following year. In the western zones, former concentration camps such as Dachau, Neuengamme, Flossenbürg, and Esterwegen were also used to house German suspects, including suspected war criminals and camp guards, but conditions in them, though unpleasant, were never as harsh as in the Soviet special camps. This was because the latter were tools of the social reorganization that the communists were engineering in Eastern Europe, by which 'antifascist democracy' would emerge on the basis of the destruction of the bourgeoisie as a class. By early 1950, the special camps' useful life span had ended and, now for the most part empty of DPs and German suspects, they either fell into disrepair or became museums.

One of the characteristics of the Soviet special camps that allowed the Soviets to act with impunity was the camps' 'colonial setting'. The Soviet occupation zone, later the GDR, was the westernmost outpost of Stalin's desire to establish 'friendly regimes' on the Soviet Union's borders. In the German case, Soviet security—that is, not having to fear a German invasion—was absolutely crucial. Even though there was a sizeable domestic support for communism, unlike in, say, Romania, nevertheless the process of Stalinization (as opposed merely to communization) meant that German communist leaders who had been trained in Moscow and would do Moscow's bidding were essential. The country became essentially a Soviet colony.

The point is worth making because in colonial settings, as we saw in Chapter 2, the tendency of the metropole to abandon the rule of law and to create and 'manage' superfluous populations is clear. The Jews in Cyprus got off lightly by comparison with the victims of British and French colonial violence in other settings, most notably in Kenya and Algeria. In both cases, concentration camps were employed to terrible effect.

Strikingly, several authors refer to the 'Gulag' in the context of the Mau Mau uprising in Kenya. More people were detained in Kenya than anywhere else in the British Empire, with a maximum of 71,346 detained in December 1954, the vast majority of them (98 per cent) from Kenya's Kikuyu-speaking central highlands. Historian David Anderson calculates that 'at least one in four Kikuyu adult males were imprisoned or detained by the British colonial administration at some time between 1952 and 1958'. Kenya already had a higher number of prisoners than neighbouring British colonies of Uganda and Tanganyika, but when the 'Emergency' began in 1952 it increased rapidly. As part of Operation Anvil in 1954, further camps were built, and the use of forced labour—contrary to international law—was sanctioned by Oliver Lyttleton, Secretary of State for the Colonies in Churchill's Tory government. Operation Anvil itself was 'Gestapolike', as loudspeakers were set up in Nairobi and a 25,000-strong security force cordoned off the city to search it sector by sector in order to 'purge' it, a technique that the British had previously deployed in Tel Aviv.

The camps emptied out quite rapidly as of 1955, but by the end of 1958, 4,688 so-called 'hard core cases' who had refused to confess to being part of the Mau Mau movement were still being held. Almost all of them were held under the Emergency Powers on suspicion of supporting the Mau Mau and were never formally charged. Anderson, building on work done by other scholars, claims that the description of the Kenyan camps as 'a Kenyan Gulag' is 'tellingly accurate' (see Figure 8). Violence was routine,

8. One of the Mau Mau camps.

torture commonplace, the British guards were not properly trained and could do what they liked, disease was rife, and the demand that prisoners confess before they could be 'rehabilitated' smacks of Kafkaesque communist 're-education' routines. Prisoners were routinely humiliated and deprived of food; as one, Nderi Kagombe, writes, 'We would be starved for as many as six or seven days; then Mapiga ["the beater", the nickname of the guard] would have the *askaris* bring in huge quantities of porridge and force us to eat it. Having not eaten for so long, it was very painful' (cited in Elkins). Historian Caroline Elkins controversially writes that the Kenyan camps 'were not wholly different from those in Nazi Germany or Stalinist Russia' and suggests, provocatively, that in these camps (known as the 'Pipeline') 'Britain finally revealed the true nature of its civilizing mission.' The slogan placed at the entrance to Aguthi Camp read: 'He Who Helps Himself Will Also Be Helped.'

The extent of the torture and brutal rule that characterized the British camps in Kenya has become clearer in the last decade. The same is true of the camp system established by the French in the context of the Algerian War (1954–62). In France, however, the difficult discussions about Algeria have been going on for longer; unlike Kenya, Algeria was administered as a part of mainland France, not a colony, and the fight to retain it united almost all shades of French political opinion. During the years of the war, some 2.3 million people were driven out of their villages and 'resettled' in some 2,000 *camps de regroupement*—in other words, a third of the rural population. The inmates depended on the army for their basic necessities, the hygiene conditions were appalling, and one historian notes that they were no more than 'fenced-in tent camps'. After 1958, with de Gaulle's return to power, plans to improve conditions and turn the camps into 'new villages' were announced but by 1962 only very few had been built. Unsurprisingly, the camps which were supposed to stem support for guerrillas—in Kenya, Algeria, and many other examples from Rhodesia to Vietnam—had the opposite effect. And where resettlement succeeded, as in Malaya, 'it usually did so not because of any economic benefits it generated for a majority, but through sheer force', as historian Christian Gerlach reminds us.

French plans to create 'new villages' were echoes of other colonial settings. In Malaya, for example, the British tried to separate the communist guerrillas from the jungle inhabitants through forced resettlement plans. The 1952 Briggs Plan envisaged moving 570,000 peasants and 'squatters' to 480 enclosed new villages. The plan's remit was not just military: it also foresaw a reorganization of Malaya's socio-economic structure, in particular the integration of the Chinese population into the rural economy. In Kenya, the colonial authorities intended something similar. Called 'villagization', the plan to resettle the Kikuyu population in some 800 barbed-wire enclosed camps and villages was one of the main drivers of the Mau Mau uprising.

It was ironic, to say the least, to see the armies of the liberal democracies—not least that of France, which regarded itself as the heir to the French Resistance, and that of Britain, which prided itself on defeating fascism—using violence involving carpet bombing, expulsions, massacres of civilians, and torture in attempts to suppress anti-colonial movements. And the use of camps during this process was most distressing of all for anyone who associated the liberal democracies with the liberation of camps, not with running them. As the historian Moritz Feichtinger says, 'Nowhere was the universal promise of human rights more unmasked as rhetoric and nowhere did late colonialism reveal its murderous face as plainly as in its use of internment and torture, which took place in a broadly-spread out camp system.'

Communist camps

As we have seen (Chapter 4), in the post-Stalinist Soviet Union, although a huge number of Gulag inmates were released, the camps continued to exist with a focus more squarely on political dissidents. Across the communist world, camps remained in force. For a brief period they 'flowered' in the newly acquired satellite states of Eastern Europe but they were most willingly employed further east, in the newer communist countries of China and Cambodia.

Perhaps the most notorious of the East European communist prison camps was established in Romania. In that country, communism had almost no local support and had to be brutally imposed. Tens of thousands of Romanians were deported to camps or to work on slave labour construction projects, most infamously the Danube–Black Sea Canal. The years 1958–62 were ones of 'blind, paroxystic repression', according to Joël Kotek and Pierre Rigoulot, with mass arrests, deportations, and executions. 180,000 Romanians were in camps in the 1950s. But even before that, one particular prison had become, in the years 1949–52, the site of some of the most gruesome experiments with human beings. In Piteşti, a draconian scheme known as 're-education by torture' was introduced, whereby political prisoners, mostly former members of Romania's fascist Iron Guard, were offered freedom from prison and employment in the security forces if they would torture fellow prisoners and extract information from them. Led by Eugen Ţurcanu, a group of torturers put this process into action on 6 December 1949. The numbers killed were small—thirty in Piteşti and thirty-four others at other prisons—but many hundreds more were tortured; the process was only stopped when the Western press got wind of it and, in order to dissociate itself from the outrageous actions, the communist authorities tried and executed Ţurcanu and seventeen others.

But the clearest instantiation of the communist camp logic was found in Democratic Kampuchea, that is, Cambodia under Khmer Rouge (KR) rule from 1975 to 1979. It is no exaggeration to say that the KR aimed—and to a large extent succeeded—in turning Cambodia as a whole into a giant concentration camp. This aim did not emerge out of nowhere, a murderous political project in a historical vacuum. Cambodia was caught up in the Vietnam War, with the US Air Force dropping 2,756,941 tons of bombs on the country, much of it indiscriminately. The bombing, according to one Yale University report, 'drove an enraged populace into the arms of an insurgency that had enjoyed relatively little support until the bombing began, setting in motion the expansion of the Vietnam War deeper into Cambodia, a coup d'état in 1970, the rapid rise of the Khmer Rouge, and ultimately the Cambodia genocide'. With what we might call their 'Stalinist-peasantist-fascist' ideology—a mixture of ultra-collectivization, a rejection of city life and worship of cultivation, and an obsession with Cambodia's 'glorious past', the Khmer Rouge closed Cambodia off from the rest of the world. Democratic Kampuchea cleared the cities, demonized the so-called 'new people' who lived in them (in contrast to the 'base people' who worked the land), rejected anything to do with the Western world, from industrial technology to the wearing of glasses, murdered non-Khmer minority groups, and forced an inhumane system of communal living on its people. At the heart of this cruel and superstitious system was an actual camp: Tuol Sleng or S21. A mark of the regime's paranoia, the camp was where Khmer Rouge cadres were tortured on suspicion of being Vietnamese agents—naturally without any basis for the fear—before being executed at Choeung Ek, the 'killing fields' ten miles south-east of Phnom Penh. Only a handful of people are known to have survived Tuol Sleng; some 14,000 were murdered there. Its existence in the midst of a giant camp (Cambodia) tells us what the system could be distilled down to: fear, paranoia, self-destruction, and extreme violence. Its commandant, Kaing Guek Eav, known as Comrade Duch, claimed that 'We were destroying the old world in order to build a new one. We wanted to manufacture a new conception of the world.' Cambodia's extreme case illustrates the ultimate logic of concentration camps: causing destruction in the name of creation.

The Khmer Rouge's self-destructive ideology was exposed when Vietnamese troops occupied the country in 1979 and the first foreigners to see Cambodia for four years were readmitted. In China, by contrast, the camp system has remained largely out of sight—to foreigners—for decades, rightly being termed the 'forgotten archipelago' by Jean-Luc Domenach. China, write Philip Williams and Yenna Wu, the authors of one study of the camp system, 'endured more than its share of concentration camps during the 20th century. Moreover,' they go on, 'China is the only major world power to have entered the 21st century with a thriving concentration camp system, which has been commonly known as "the laogai system" [*laodong gaizao zhidu*] since May 1951.' Of course, in China one cannot refer to 'concentration camps', only to 'remoulding through labour facilities' or 're-education through labour facilities'. The term 'concentration camp' is freely used by emigrants who have published their memoirs abroad, as one might expect; but scholars have also found the term applicable. 'While considerable variability among the camps is naturally present in a country as large and diverse as China,' Williams and Wu write, 'the living and working conditions in their camps have often evoked the harshness associated with concentration camps, particularly during spikes in the death rate such as the record-breaking famine of 1959–62.'

As in the Soviet Union, the *laogai* system has also been characterized by the forced settlement of those formally 'freed' from the camps. When Harry Wu, who has done more than any other former inmate to bring the *laogai* to the attention of Westerners, returned to China in 1991 to make a film about the camps for CBS, he met a former prisoner named Zhou. Having served eight years from 1956 to 1964 for 'counterrevolutionary crimes', Zhou then remained in Xining, the capital of Qinghai province, for a further twenty-seven years. He told Wu that one third of the province's population were resettlement prisoners and their families. 'Their labour', writes Wu, 'had been used, he told me, to reclaim wasteland, construct roads, open up mines, and build dams, not just prior to 1979 but throughout the 1980s.' In other words, more so than in the Soviet Union, the labour of *laogai* prisoners was economically beneficial to the Chinese Communist Party; the goods manufactured by the prisoners 'are sold in domestic as well as foreign markets and have become an indispensable component of the national economy'. This claim is hardly surprising when one considers the numbers involved. In 1992, Harry Wu estimated that at least fifty million people had been sentenced to labour reform camps over the previous forty years and that sixteen to twenty million were still confined in them. Thought reform through labour turned out to be a convenient way of acquiring 'a dependable source of wealth', as Luo Ruiqing, the Public Security Minister, put it at the Communist general assembly of 1954. The *laogai* system was formally abolished in 2013 but the structure of the system remains: prison factories, psychiatric prisons, community correction centres, and other forms of extrajudicial incarceration all still exist, according to campaigners.

Although it seems likely that prison camps still exist in China, the last major communist camp system is that in North Korea. It remains very difficult to acquire reliable information but there is no doubt that a network of concentration camps holding some 150,000–200,000 people exists in that country, camps which are likely to become increasingly harsh as the country heads ever more towards catastrophe. One of the few memoirs by a former inmate is Kang Chol-hwan's *The Aquariums of Pyongyang*. Following his grandfather's arrest, Chol-hwan's family (apart from his mother, the daughter of a 'heroic family') was deported to Yodok camp as the family of a criminal. Although, he says, the case could seem like one of 'simple banishment' to a place where those 'contaminated' by the proximity of a criminal could be 'redeemed', in fact 'the barbed wire, the huts, the malnutrition, and the mind-quashing work left little doubt that it really was a concentration camp'. Chol-hwan was to spend ten years growing up in the camp. What did he learn?

> The only lesson I got pounded into me was about man's limitless capacity for vice—that and the fact that social distinctions vanish in a concentration camp. I once believed that man was different from other animals, but Yodok showed me that reality doesn't support this opinion. In the camp, there was no difference between man and beast, except maybe that a very hungry human was capable of stealing food from its little ones while an animal, perhaps, was not. I also saw many people die in the camp, and their deaths looked like that of other animals.

(*Aquariums of Pyongyang*, p. 160)

Sadly, these communist camps are by no means the last examples of concentration camps in the modern world. Camps existed in the right-wing dictatorships of Argentina and Chile and, tellingly, in the context of the genocide in Bosnia, where images of Omarska and Trnopolje opened the world's eyes to the fact that what was taking place in the wars of Yugoslav succession was not merely 'typical Balkan tribalism'. The Wikipedia entry for 'list of concentration and internment camps' has entries for over forty different countries, including Sweden, Sri Lanka, and Montenegro as well as the more obvious examples.

This chapter has shown just some of the many locations in which concentration camps, or sites like concentration camps, have existed since the Second World War. The evidence suggests first, that concentration camps constitute a world-wide phenomenon which has developed over time as different states and regimes have learned from others in other parts of the world and, second, that these institutions, especially because they emerge in different settings under very different political regimes, tell us something fundamental about modernity and about the modern state. Precisely what that 'something' is will be the subject of the final chapter.

Chapter 6
'An Auschwitz every three months': society as camp?

Camps as warning?

In 2015, newspapers were reporting that part of the former concentration camp of Dachau (the 'herb garden'—not part of the memorial museum) was being used to house refugees. The people whose refugee camp is one of the world's most notorious former concentration camps are among the lucky ones. Other refugee camps in countries bordering Syria and in cities across Europe are holding 'migrants'—as the press likes to call them—whose future prospects look much less promising. One might argue that the 'refugee crisis' itself in its European context is a rhetorical construct; it certainly seems bizarre that whilst countries like Lebanon and Jordan have each taken in over 1 million Syrian refugees, European countries are apparently unable to cope with tens of thousands.

Are these refugee camps in Dachau or elsewhere concentration camps or even akin to them? The people forced to live in them clearly do not want to be there; the experience is humiliating. A 2009 Human Rights Watch report on refugee centres in Libya, whose construction Italy paid for, described 'inhuman and degrading conditions' inside them. At the same time as the refugees can expect a minimum of care, it is also quite clear to them that

9. 'Freedom Thru Detention', Dave Brown cartoon, *Independent*, 19 April 2000.

they are an unwanted population. The camps are there both to aid people who have had to flee their homes and to provide sites of their exclusion from the 'world of nations' (see Figure 9). Should we be alarmed that the 21st century is again going to become a century of camps?

The matter is complex. There is no single type of concentration camp and no clear dividing line between a concentration camp and other sites of incarceration. If one searches book titles, one can find books that deal with the 'South Korean Gulag', the 'Chilean Gulag', the 'Israeli Gulag', the 'Hungarian Gulag', and many other supposed cases. The massive growth of California's prison system is called by one analyst a 'Golden Gulag' because the 'prison boom' has seen a jump in incarceration rates of 450 per cent since 1980. This huge growth is partly a result of what some civil rights groups such as the American Civil Liberties Union refer to as the 'school-to-prison-pipeline', which refers to the ways in which poorer and more vulnerable children in the US are driven along a disciplinary trajectory heading for prison rather than education. There is even a book dealing with the 'Gulag of the family courts'. Clearly the concentration camp image is good propaganda. We need to tread carefully. We also need to note, however, that some philosophers and sociologists have been quite outspoken with respect to the significance of concentration camps for understanding 21st century societies. It is a greater source of concern for today's world to think about the growth and variety of camps than it is to prove that any one particular type of prison or camp system merits the term 'gulag'.

For example, the idea that there are connections between historical concentration camps and contemporary sites or territories of incarceration receives scholarly backing from the Italian philosopher Giorgio Agamben, who makes his claim by bringing together Michel Foucault's concept of 'biopower' (the ability of the state to decide on the life and death of its citizens) and German legal philosopher (and Nazi) Carl Schmitt's concept of the 'state of exception'. Agamben argues that the camp has replaced the city as the biopolitical paradigm of the West. For Agamben the historian's question as to whether camps originated in Cuba or South Africa is less important than understanding that camps have become 'the most absolute *conditio inhumana* that has ever existed on earth' and that rather than being a purely historical datum or an anomaly in human history, they are in some way 'the hidden matrix and *nomos* of the political space in which we are still living'. Agamben defines the concentration camp thus: 'The camp is the space that is opened when the state of exception begins to become the rule.' Where the state of exception was once sparingly used to suspend the rule of law temporarily at a moment of emergency, the camp marks the point at which the state of exception 'is now given a permanent spatial arrangement, which as such nevertheless remains outside the normal order'.

Agamben's arguments have been very influential, with critics taking his definition as a starting point for examining all manner of institutions and developments in domestic and international law, not least the US's suspension of the rule of law in holding people without charge in Guantánamo Bay. Agamben himself uses his theories to protest against biometrical data gathering, seeing it as a way for the state to extend its biopolitical reach, effectively making suspects out of citizens. Others have used the arguments about the spatialization and normalization of the concept of the state of exception to argue that the concentration camp is nowadays not an aberration but the norm. Whole swathes of territory, in this reading, might be considered 'states of exception', places where inhabitants have been abandoned by the rule of law and which are thus effectively concentration camps. What looks at first glance like a metaphor designed to awaken us to the cruel realities of many people's lives might turn out to be a simple description of fact.

On the other hand, Agamben has been criticized for disregarding facts, making out of a vast panoply of camps—there was, as Nikolaus Wachsmann reminds us, no typical concentration camp in the Third Reich—an icon, 'the camp'. This is not merely made to do service as an archetypal concentration camp, it supposedly tells us something about the inner life and logic of the modern state as such. Agamben makes the fact that the Nazis ruled according to Article 48 of the Weimar constitution—permitting rule by decree in exceptional circumstances—into a general rule of the modern world: that the 'state of exception' is increasingly becoming the norm, used as a means of suspending democratic politics (whilst formally retaining the liberal constitution) and controlling populations. One critic, the philosopher Ichiro Takayoshi, objects that Agamben's attempt to find 'the platonic form of the camp' means that he transposes a legal concept—the state of exception, in which the exception, which is outside the norm, is included in the norm as a conceptual possibility—into the realm of the Nazi camps, where it does not apply. The inmates of the camps were not simultaneously inside and outside the law; rather, as Takayoshi says, they were simply designated as enemies, then 'denationalized' by having legal protection withdrawn, before finally being concentrated and/or eliminated in the camp system. The facts of the matter do not seem to support Agamben's claim to have seen in camps of all sorts 'the *nomos* of the modern'. Camps might indeed be embodiments of a state of exception because they represent a suspension of the law but it does not follow that the state of exception is the leitmotif of Western political culture.

Nevertheless, camps of all sorts do continue to exist today. Even if we do not subscribe to Agamben's position, does anything unite refugee camps, IDP camps, migrant holding camps (such as Dachau's herb garden, Mineo in Sicily, or Bela near Prague), makeshift refugee camps such as the former 'Jungle' in Calais or sport stadiums in Athens, or detention centres for asylum seekers such as Yarl's Wood in Oxford or Colnbrook near Heathrow Airport? In considering this question, Agamben's insight that camps—or rather, those held in them—represent the deployment of the 'state of exception' is helpful, for it assists us in thinking through what a concentration camp is, where the state of exception is explicit and intended, and what might better be thought of as places where people are held against their will but where the state of exception is not, or is only partially, enforced (if that metaphor of a 'partial state of exception' makes sense).

Agamben's argument can also help with considering the question of how development intersects with the existence of camps. It is true that the number of people existing on less than $1.25 a day has halved in the last twenty-five years, from 1.9 billion to 836 million. Global poverty is something that people care about, although there is a paradox in rich countries offering even relatively large amounts in aid to countries whose poverty is structurally entrenched by the trade policies and consumption patterns of those same rich countries. Questions about the ethics of development aid are beyond the scope of this book, however.

What interests me here is the question of whether there is anything to be learned about the contemporary world by asking this question: do the inhabitants of the 'global south' (what used to be called the Third World) live in a giant concentration camp?

This most capacious understanding of what constitutes a concentration camp is put forward by Vinay Lal, who claims that the global south's inhabitants are effectively slave labourers producing cheap goods to satisfy the rich countries' consumerist obsessions, the victims of an invisible genocide. Historically one can find evidence that lends some support to this view. As we have seen in examples from South Africa, Cuba, and the Philippines at the turn of the 20th century, and Kenya, Malaya, and Algeria after the Second World War, 'destruction and "development", the emptying of some areas and the stabilization, improved control over, and exploitation of others, were two sides of the same coin in anti-guerrilla warfare', as Christian Gerlach writes. Schemes for 'villagization' or the control of the jungle in Malaya or Kenya were premised on stemming support for guerrillas and 'modernizing' the country. In Lal's reading, the argument is taken further: 'development' is genocide and the people who service its institutions are dwellers in the world's largest concentration camps. Ironically, in contrast to practitioners of 'open genocide, who may have to face the gallows or the humiliation of trial before an international tribunal, the stalwarts of this form of ethnic cleansing are often feted for their humanitarian contributions to human welfare'.

Philosopher Alfonso Lingis makes an equally provocative argument when, in trying to shock readers into realizing the realities of life for people in what would today be called the 'developing world', he argues that the 'forty thousand children dying each day in the fetid slums of Third World cities' constitutes 'an Auschwitz every three months'. The reference is made in passing in the context of a passage where Lingis argues that one has to 'speak for the silenced'; it is not a cogent, worked-through comparison.

Quite the contrary: it is Lingis's anger which jolts the reader into considering whether the comparison can and should be made at all.

Lal's and Lingis's positions are nothing if not thought-provoking. But is it really the case that the global south exists in a state of exception? Structural and institutionalized poverty, ossified through clientelist relations of dependence on Western capital, creates a harsh reality, but the camp terminology—being abandoned by the law or excluded from the ethical universe—does not do justice to the complexities of the relationships that characterize the 'world system'. There are, for example, lawyers, NGOs, and politicians able and willing to represent the inhabitants of the global south, just as they are able to mobilize and represent themselves. As a metaphor for a life that is restricted, without limited hope for improvement, and a feeling of being trapped in a position of dependence and reliance on unseen 'masters', the idea of the global south as camp contains echoes of the colonial past that give us cause for concern. But perhaps Agamben's argument is more useful when we turn to the variety of camps—in the stricter sense of enclosed sites holding people who do not wish to be there—that exist in the world today. Are concentration camps a warning for our world? In order to address this question we need to consider what camps mean in the modern age.

The meaning of camps

Sociologist Zygmunt Bauman has claimed that in the same way that the 18th century was the century of reason and the 19th that of industry, so the 20th century was the 'century of camps'. Far from being irruptions of medieval barbarism or irrationality, Bauman argues that concentration camps were not only products of modernity—means–ends thinking, technological knowhow, bureaucracy, division of labour, professionalization, control over nature, and human nature specifically—but had their own 'sinister rationality'. They performed three vital jobs: as laboratories to explore new techniques of domination; as schools for cruelty; and as 'swords over the heads of those remaining on the other side of the barbed-wire fence', who would thus remain quiescent for fear of ending up in a camp themselves. These claims can be supported by the empirical literature on Nazi Germany, the Soviet Union, and other situations where concentration camps have been deployed. But Bauman goes further and makes the camps into a synecdoche of the modern world. 'The camps,' he writes:

> were distillations of an essence diluted elsewhere, condensations of totalitarian domination and its corollary, the superfluity of man, in a pure form difficult or impossible to achieve elsewhere. The camps were patterns and blueprints for the totalitarian society, that modern dream of total order, domination, and mastery run wild, cleansed of the last vestiges of that wayward and unpredictable human freedom, spontaneity and unpredictability that held it back. The camps were testing grounds for societies run as concentration camps.
>
> ('A Century of Camps?', pp. 274–5)

This is a sort of sociological rendering of Agamben's philosophical argument that concentration camps reveal the hidden truth of the modern world. Unlike Agamben, however, Bauman sees camps as *one* logical culmination of modernity rather than the necessary expression of the truth of the modern state per se—a position which has left many perplexed by Agamben's seeming pessimism and apparent unwillingness to distinguish between totalitarian and democratic societies. In Bauman's view, the camps were invented to control human nature and—following Arendt—to make human beings superfluous. They were thus products or logical outcomes of Enlightenment thinking since the dream of mastery over nature is precisely an Enlightenment dream. This means that for Bauman camps go hand in hand with modernity; they are the clearest expression of the modern state's potential for domination.

In some ways, Bauman is quite right: as we have seen most clearly with the Gulag, camps often go hand in hand with social restructuring or, more relevantly, breakneck economic development. The conveniently timed programme of *dekulakization* allowed the 1929 order to expand the special settlements to take effect; thereafter economic modernization and concentration camps went hand in hand in the Soviet Union. In that sense, Bauman is correct to note that concentration camps are not radically separated from 'normal' society but a logical extension of it. Concentration camps are thus 'total institutions', as described by sociologist Erving Goffman, places such as monasteries, asylums, or prisons where those inside are tightly regulated, sometimes involuntarily, by specific rules. Those inside the 'total institution' can adapt, according to Goffman, in one of four ways: regression (retreating into the self), resistance (actively fighting the system), colonization (learning to cope in the institution), or conversion (adopting the mentality of the guards). On this reading, concentration camps are like ordinary society in that certain rules apply and inmates' ability to survive depends on how well they can adapt their pre-existing values and mores (what sociologist Pierre Bourdieu calls *habitus*) to the requirements of camp life.

Yet there is something oddly comforting about Bauman's argument that camps are an expression of modernity, with its stress on instrumental rationality, bureaucratic officialdom, and the divorce of the moral from the technological. There is something equally comforting about Goffman's notion of a 'total institution' that represents simply a more extreme, repressive version of familiar institutions. Both theories permit a critique of rules of socialization, science, and rationality that shields us from the more violent and wild aspects of this history. Their focus is more on a critique of society than on understanding concentration camps.

There are arguments in Bauman's favour: when one looks at camps in colonial settings, one can easily argue that they represent the power of the modern state enforcing its rule on unwilling 'natives', even if such policies actually testify to the colonial state's weakness in terms of its ability to rule effectively—the turn to force indicates a lack of legitimacy. In the Soviet Union, one can show that economic modernization and the Gulag were inseparable. Only after the Stalinist period, when more technical industries became significant, were the armies of forced woodcutters and railway builders surplus to requirements. In many cases, such as Franco's Spain, terror went hand in hand with the notion that work would redeem the 'feeble-minded Reds'. In the case of Bosnia, however, the camps served no purpose except terror; in the Third Reich concentration camps served different purposes at different times: terror and the elimination of real or possible opposition; getting rid of 'asocial elements'; holding foreign POWs, especially politically suspect persons; involvement in the Holocaust; slave labour. In all cases, including in Kenya, Malaya, and Algeria, concentration camps have an air of madness about them that is not captured by Bauman's description.

In the abstract, concentration camps might appear to be the logical conclusion of modernity, if by that is meant an indefinite extension of state power and a belief in 'scientific' solutions to social 'problems'. But apart from the fact that from the Soviet Union to the Nazi war economy slave labour cost more to administer than it produced, concentration camps have always been about more than modernization. They are places of punishment, of discipline, where specific regimes' world views are actualized. These world views need not be 'modern' in Bauman's sense, which equates modernity with technology and bureaucracy. Rather, they are 'modern' in the sense that the modern age also intensified and canalized paranoid fantasies about racial and political 'others'—ideas which long predated the modern age but which were expressed in new ways under modern conditions. Concentration camps, as Arendt noted, are places of terror, experiments in eradicating 'the human' from human beings. Camps are tools of the modern state but they are hardly the most 'rational' use of resources or the most logical tool of nation-building. There is something else going on.

That something else is the way in which the terror of concentration camps exceeds their rational use and even the thought-out desire for terror and revenge on the part of those who create them. There is an aspect of concentration camps that simply cannot be captured by describing them as manifestations of 'absolute power' or as the '*nomos* of the modern'. The camp is a product of modernity but also embodies a desire to overthrow rationality: a desire to abandon all limits, to transgress the moral law, and to engage in a kind of organized frenzy. This madness of the camps is such that even good communists reached instinctively for the theological terminology: as Eugenia Ginzburg left her first prison, she noted that from the time of her arrest: 'Everything since then had consisted only of my wanderings through hell. Or could it be purgatory?'

This is where we can see similarities but also crucial differences between sweatshops, internment camps for asylum seekers, and refugee camps on the one hand and concentration camps in violent colonial and totalitarian states on the other, with places like Guantánamo Bay, an extraterritorial site where the law has been suspended, falling somewhere in between. The fact is that there is no simple definition of concentration camps; rather, they exist on a continuum of carceral practices, including detention centres, internment camps, prisons, ghettos, leper colonies, asylums, and other sites of exclusion. It is probable that practices developed in one have been learned and adapted in others—some authors claim, for example, that CIA practices in Guantánamo derive from torture practices first used in Nazi camps.

Yet the fact that we might be offended by, for example, the herding of illegal immigrants into a stadium (as the Italian police did in 1991 with Albanians) or by *zones d'attentes* in French airports should not mislead us into thinking that Bari or Charles de Gaulle Airport are equivalent to Auschwitz. Likewise, the inhabitants of Gaza are trapped in a territory that they ultimately do not control and where they suffer all manner of deprivations; but calling the

Gaza Strip a concentration camp is actually a lazy way of trying
to capture the specific nature of the day-to-day negotiation of
power between Israeli occupation and supposed Palestinian
self-government—the state of exception is a regularly imposed but
not permanent feature of life there. The inhabitants of asylum
seekers' detention centres are removed from the human 'circle of
obligation'; they are treated, in Arendt's terms, as if they no longer
exist. But the rule of law has not entirely been suspended in their
case. It is certainly objectionable that people who have fled their
countries and are already highly vulnerable should be locked up
and treated as suspects instead of being permitted to contribute to
the country in which they are seeking asylum; the fact that they
sometimes have to wait for years before being either released or
deported is shameful and is an abuse of legal process. They are very
close to falling into Arendt's category of the superfluous stateless
person from whom 'the right to have rights' has been removed.
But not quite: they can be legally represented and the law which
mocks them sometimes also produces decisions in their favour.
Thus, even if we want to retain the name 'concentration camps'
to describe all of the institutions discussed in this book—from the
South African camps to the Gulag to Guantánamo—we have to
recognize that the term encompasses a multitude of realities.
Concentration camps throughout the 20th and 21st centuries
are by no means all the same, with respect either to the degree
of violence that characterizes them or the extent to which
their inmates are abandoned by the authorities. And if we do not
want to use the term so liberally, it is important that that decision
should not be taken to mean that we condone institutions that
we do not consider to be concentration camps.

The crucial characteristic of a concentration camp is not whether
it has barbed wire, fences, or watchtowers; it is, rather, the
gathering of civilians, defined by a regime as de facto 'enemies', in
order to hold them against their will without charge in a place
where the rule of law has been suspended. Internment camps for
political prisoners and detention centres for asylum seekers are

places where those inside are held against their will but not places, at least in theory, where the law does not apply—although it might well be bent somewhat. Even Guantánamo, which is regularly called a concentration camp, can at least be criticized by lawyers and human rights campaigners in the US and elsewhere. But the difference is one of degree, and as we have seen in this book, whose examples range from vast 'special settlements' without fixed border fences to death camps, any attempt to provide a fixed definition quickly runs into problems, even as we can see that such places cannot simply be reduced to 'the same'. We are returned to Arendt's theological continuum of Hades, purgatory, and hell: we can see that some camps are worse than others, but unlike in Arendt's scheme (purgatory and hell are separate realms, even if one can move between them) it is not clear exactly where one sort of camp merges with the next.

What is missing from Bauman's description of concentration camps—as opposed to any of the other sort of institutions discussed here—is the absence of rationality that one finds alongside 'modern' structures. 'Hier ist kein warum' (There is no why here) responded a guard to Primo Levi when he prevented Levi from sucking on an icicle in Auschwitz; the absurd accusations—bourgeois wrecking and the like—that filled up the Soviet Gulag are just as preposterous. We need an analysis which combines the 'how' of the concentration camps (bureaucracy, rationality, and so on) with the 'why' they are there in the first place (paranoid fears of fifth columnists, race traitors, and so on). In concentration camps there is a seemingly insane abandonment of reality accompanied by the most brutal and unceasing reminders to the inmates that what they are suffering is inescapably real. In terms of accusations and judgements we are in the realm of the fantastical; in terms of punishment, in the all too human realm of a harsh reality.

In 1949, American critic Isaac Rosenfeld published an article in *Partisan Review* entitled 'The Meaning of Terror'. In this cry of despair, Rosenfeld set out his opinion that the world had been forever sullied:

> Terror is today the main reality, because it is the model reality. The concentration camp is the model educational system and the model form of government. War is the model enterprise and the model form of communality. These are abstract propositions, but even so they are obvious; when we fill them in with experience they are overwhelming.
>
> (*Preserving the Hunger*, p. 133)

What does it mean to say that the concentration camp is the 'model form of government'? Surely this is no more than a case of post-war shock? And yet the recurrence of concentration camps, states' ready recourse to them in all parts of the world in different political, geographical, and cultural settings, suggests that Rosenfeld might have been on to something.

What Rosenfeld captured was the way in which the concentration camp became an expression of modern states at a certain moment in time. The German philosopher Karl Jaspers wrote that:

> This reality of concentration camps, this circular movement of torturers and tortures, this loss of humanity threatens human survival in the future. Confronted with the reality of the concentration camps, we are unable to speak. This is a greater danger than the atom bomb, since it represents a threat to the human soul (cited in Ivanova).

That may be true but it is also ahistorical. Concentration camps emerged in the early 20th century as modern states emerged out of older empires, sustained by ideas of nationalism and biological metaphors defining the healthy and valuable on the one hand and the polluting and degenerate on the other.

It is in fact possible to historicize the emergence of the concentration camp and to explain why, for all the continuities with social and colonial practices of preceding centuries, the term and the phenomenon arose when they did. The concept of the concentration camp, Javier Rodrigo reminds us, 'refers not so much to a place with a set of uniform features over space and time as to the *status* that has been conferred on such a place'. As he notes, concentration camps emerged in many places around the same time, but with distinct local variations, meaning that there is a 'cumulative history' of concentration camps, 'with lessons learned, discontinuities and adaptations to the contexts in which they developed'. Rodrigo provides a clear statement of the context in which concentration camps emerged in the wake of colonial wars and the First World War:

> The concentration camps symbolized the transformation and radicalization of the politics of occupation, which extended from the treatment of political prisoners and prisoners of war to the deportation of civilians, from forced labour in extreme conditions to the hunger and misery occupied peoples were also subjected to. Concentration camps also came to serve as a space for social cleansing and internal politics.
> ('Exploitation, Fascist Violence', p. 563)

Concentration camps were ways of keeping the unwanted elements at bay and, furthermore, putting them to use: not only through their labour (which was rarely very productive) but as a warning to wider society too. 'The camp,' Richard Overy writes, 'reflected political and social insecurities, and a public discourse of fear, part real, part sustained by regimes built on warring ideologies.' The concentration camp was an expression of the centralization of terror, one of the key characteristics of the modern state in the age of nationalism and technology.

The memory of the camps

When British troops arrived at Belsen, not only did they liberate the camp but they also filmed that liberation. The ceasefire negotiations on 15 April 1945 were recorded by the British Army

Film and Photographic Unit (AFPU), and the next day it began a planned two-week coverage on Belsen. In fact, many members of the unit stayed longer, producing what Rainer Schulze has called 'a large collection of what constitutes some of the most amazing, moving and at the same time distressing images of the Second World War'. The film of the liberation was never completed and has recently been restored and finished by the Imperial War Museum in London, and released with its original title, *German Concentration Camps Factual Survey*. The sober title reflects the serious nature of the contents, and the decision to restore it and complete the work of the unit tells us that the memory of Belsen, and the Nazi camps in general, remains as strong in contemporary European culture as it has been since the end of the war.

This is a reminder that concentration camps have an afterlife. As we have seen, some of the Nazi camps were used again as DP camps or camps for political prisoners; others fell into disrepair and were ignored by the locals. But over time, many were turned into museums so that today there is still a landscape of camps across Europe, only now they are tourist sites or *Gedenkstätten*—sites of warning and contemplation. This process of musealization has always been contested, and former camp sites' meanings change over time. Buchenwald, for example, was turned by the communist authorities into the GDR's premier memorial to anti-fascism, its monuments depicting the solidarity of the underground communist resistance and perpetuating the myth of the camp's 'auto-liberation' from Nazi rule—a myth because the role of the US Army was crucial. In Auschwitz, the 'national memorials' in the main camp (Auschwitz I) were used by the communist countries to defend their anti-fascist record—even countries which were allied to Germany—and by the Austrians to promote the lie that they were the 'first victims of National Socialism' rather than enthusiastic supports of Hitler. Camps are not set in aspic; they continue to evolve as debates over restoration, 'authenticity', and changing exhibitions compete with the pressing need for tourist facilities.

The Nazi camps, more than any others, have been represented in every genre of art. From serious documentary (*The World at War*; *The Nazis: A Warning from History*) to children's films (*Chicken Run*) and TV drama (*Band of Brothers*), to novels and poetry, ranging from the restrained and severe (Ida Fink, Paul Celan, Dan Pagis) to the sensationalist (*Sophie's Choice*), children's books (*Billy the Kid*, *The Boy in the Striped Pyjamas*), comics (*Maus*, *Rain*, the Auschwitz Museum's *Episodes from Auschwitz* publications, and many didactic as well as scandalous publications), to gore fest films (*Dead Snow*, Uwe Boll's *Auschwitz*), and arthouse films (*The Grey Zone*, *Son of Saul*), to sculpture, music, and other sorts of performance, including public readings of Holocaust texts (Pinter et al.), performance art (Józef Szajna), and theatre (Tadeusz Kantor, Joshua Sobol, etc.). The camps have been depicted in Lego, in vast models (Chapman Brothers), and as backdrops to all varieties of stories and genres. Whether this ubiquitous representation of the Nazi camps constitutes a serious-minded engagement with the past or a massive banalization of it remains disputed.

What is so striking about this state of affairs is the extent to which the Nazi camps stand in for all camps. What has happened to concentration camps elsewhere? Some have been turned into museums, with a greater or lesser degree of taste. Many have disappeared altogether. The desert camp of Chacabuco in Chile was given a facelift and used as workers' barracks. Few of the camps of the Gulag have been turned into memorial sites, especially now that the Soviet Union does duty, stripped of its Stalinist ideology, as a reminder of Russian 'greatness'. In Spain, Mariano Rajoy's government stopped all funding to the associations that uncover and memorialize atrocity sites of Francoist repression in 2013. There have been efforts to memorialize camp sites in Namibia, Latin America, France, and elsewhere. But most of the concentration camps that characterized the 20th century have gone. Besides, not even all the Nazi camps are memorialized. The massive industrial facilities of Christianstadt, a sub-camp

10. Ruins at Christianstadt.

of Gross-Rosen, not far from what is today Wrocław in western Poland (formerly Breslau), are falling into ruin in the forest, largely inaccessible (see Figure 10). We remember the camps we want to remember in ways that suit us.

When the journalist Alan Moorehead published *Eclipse*, his book about the defeat of Germany in late 1945, he wrote that probably the least blameworthy of the Germans was the 'unpolitical boy' who was forced to don a uniform and fight and die for the Third Reich. 'There is only one thing possible that one can do for him now,' wrote Moorehead: 'be vigilant to snap the long chains that lead to the future Belsens before they grow too long.'

Given the history of the postwar period, we might wonder whether the world has been engaged in strengthening and tightening those long chains rather than snapping them. There seems little likelihood of future Belsens in Europe, at least for the foreseeable future—though we thought that before Omarska too. But the Chinese Cultural Revolution and Great Leap Forward, the internment of Jewish DPs illegally seeking entry into Palestine on British-controlled Cyprus, the holding of suspected anti-colonial rebels in Malaya and Kenya, the continued existence of the Gulag in the post-war Soviet Union, even in its scaled-down version, the Khmer Rouge's 'country-as-concentration camp', the rape camps of Bosnia, Guantánamo Bay's suspension of the rule of law, the still-existing North Korean camp system, to name just the most obvious, all suggest that concentration camps have not only not disappeared; they have become an all-too-ubiquitous characteristic of our world. And no surprise; we live in a world where inter-state competition encourages inter-community tensions, where 'the war on terror' breeds the thing it is supposedly suppressing, where legal protection of human rights and the commemoration of 'heroes of the Holocaust' such as Sir Nicholas Winton go hand in hand with contempt for refugees, who are pushed into makeshift camps or interned in 'detention centres'. Concentration camps are the compressed and condensed values of the state when it feels itself most threatened.

Could it be that the collective memory of the Nazi camps, cultivated in the West but now widely shared across the world and endorsed by the UN in events such as Holocaust Memorial Day (27 January, the date of the liberation of Auschwitz), has diverted our attention from other atrocities? Moorehead predicted something like this in 1945:

> A shudder of horror went round the world when the news of these concentration camps was published, but only I think because of the special interest and the special moment in the war. We were engrossed with Germany, and it is perhaps not too subtle to say that since Germany was manifestly beaten people wanted to have a justification for their fight, a proof that they were engaged against evil. From the German point of view Belsen was perfectly mistimed. Worse camps existed in Poland and we took no notice. Dachau was described in the late nineteen-thirties and we did not

want to hear. In the midst of the war three-quarters of a million
Indians starved in Bengal because shipping was wanted in other
parts, and we were bored.

The last living patient has been evacuated from Belsen. The
hateful buildings have been burned down. The physical evidence
of all those horrible places will soon have been wiped out.
Only the mental danger remains. The danger of indifference.

(*Eclipse*, p. 229)

It would be wrong to argue that Holocaust memory has been
deliberately cultivated to place the focus on suffering Jews at the
expense of others. The idea that there is a 'Holocaust industry'
is a slander against those whose enduring interest in the murder
of the Jews stems from a very human reaction to so terrible a
crime. Yet the enormity of the Nazi murder of the Jews and our
understandable fascination with it does mean that other cases of
genocide or massive human rights abuse are not always properly
understood, especially if they do not look like the Holocaust. It
means too that the term 'concentration camps' has come to denote
places like Dachau when in fact most of them were quite different,
with the result that propagandists exploit the association to
overstate the extent of 'their' suffering on the one hand, or that the
term is rejected in cases other than Nazi Germany on the other
hand. More problematic still, the proliferation of concentration
camps since the end of the Second World War suggests that
Moorehead was right: indifference towards the suffering of others
is as common now, in the age of immediately available electronic
news media, as it was between the wars. Survivor of the Nazi
camps Boris Pahor claimed that modern Europeans are 'basically
thoughtless and cowardly', that they have become used to a
comfortable existence. 'Today's standardized man,' he surmised,
'may be awakened, who knows, only by some new lay order that
dons striped camp burlaps and floods the capitals of our countries,
unsettling the complacency of shopping malls with the harsh
clatter of their wooden clogs.' The response from most of Europe's

leaders in 2015 as Syrian refugees sought assistance in fleeing one of the most destructive wars in recent history suggests that Pahor may have been too optimistic.

The majority of the world's population does not live in concentration camps—that claim is more polemic or a call to action than an accurate description of the facts. But that many commentators lay claim to the concentration camp metaphor when discussing Bangladeshi textile factories, Guantánamo Bay, the Gaza Strip, or even the global south as a whole should at least lead us to consider the inequalities that define our world and the threat of greater conflict in an age of accelerating climate change. The claim that the camp could be 'our' future or that the camp represents the secret inner workings of the modern state, if not entirely persuasive because it is ahistorical, should certainly make us pause for thought before deciding that concentration camps are the products merely of 'mad' dictators and their blind followers.

States can do bad things as well as good: they can destroy people's lives in concentration camps but they can also improve lives. They can nurture populations through education, health programmes, and access to welfare in a way that creates critically engaged citizens rather than downtrodden, suspiciously regarded subjects. There is more to the history of the 20th century than its depressing abominations in centres of detention and destruction. At the start of the 21st century one could be forgiven, however, for thinking that those beneficial aspects of the state have been severely attenuated for many of the inhabitants of our planet. And those of us who are more fortunate—who live in places where a vestige of the post-war social democratic settlement still survives—might do well to watch our backs.

References

This section includes works cited or drawn on in the text. Page numbers refer to direct quotations or specific information such as statistics, in the order they appear in the text.

Chapter 1: What is a concentration camp?

Giorgio Agamben, *Homo Sacer: Sovereign Power and Bare Life* (Stanford: Stanford University Press, 1998)

Hannah Arendt, *The Origins of Totalitarianism*, rev. edn (San Diego: Harcourt Brace & Company, 1979), 465, 457, 445

Patrick Gordon Walker, *The Lid Lifts* (London: Victor Gollancz, 1945), 65–7

Kevin Passmore, *Fascism: A Very Short Introduction* (Oxford: Oxford University Press, 2002), 29

Wolfgang Sofsky, *The Order of Terror: The Concentration Camp* (Princeton: Princeton University Press, 1997)

Trials of War Criminals before the Nuernberg Military Tribunals under Control Council Law No. 10 (NMT 'Green Series'), Vol. 5, 1067

Chapter 2: Origins

Taner Akçam, *A Shameful Act: The Armenian Genocide and the Question of Turkish Responsibility* (London: Constable, 2007), 198

Angie Debo, *A History of the Indians of the United States* (London: Pimlico, 1995), 273–6

Peter Gatrell, *A Whole Empire Walking: Refugees in Russia during World War I* (Bloomington: Indiana University Press, 1999), 200

Peter Gatrell, 'Refugees and Forced Migrants during the First World War', in Matthew Stibbe (ed.), *Captivity, Forced Labour and Forced Migration in Europe during the First World War* (London: Routledge, 2009), 86, 90, 91–2

Sheldon H. Harris, *Factories of Death: Japanese Biological Warfare, 1932–1945, and the American Cover-up*, rev. edn (New York: Routledge, 2002)

Emily Hobhouse, *The Brunt of the War and Where it Fell* (London: Methuen, 1902)

Isobel Hull, *Absolute Destruction: Military Culture and the Practices of War in Imperial Germany* (Ithaca, NY: Cornell University Press, 2004)

Jonathan Hyslop, 'The Invention of the Concentration Camp: Cuba, Southern Africa and the Philippines, 1896–1907', *South African Historical Journal*, 63:2 (2011), 260 n. 33, 257, 264

Heather Jones, 'A Missing Paradigm? Military Captivity and the Prisoner of War, 1914–18', in Matthew Stibbe (ed.), *Captivity, Forced Labour and Forced Migration in Europe during the First World War* (London: Routledge, 2009), 22

Heather Jones, 'Discipline and Punish? Forms of Violent Punishment in Prisoner of War Camps in the First World War: A Comparative Analysis', in Christoph Jahr and Jens Thiel (eds), *Lager vor Auschwitz: Gewalt und Integration im 20. Jahrhundert* (Berlin: Metropol, 2013), 100

Heather Jones, *Violence against Prisoners of War in the First World War: Britain, France and Germany, 1914–1920* (Cambridge: Cambridge University Press, 2011)

Hilmar Kaiser, *At the Crossroads of Der Zor: Death, Survival, and Humanitarian Resistance in Aleppo, 1915–1917* (Princeton and London: Gomidas Institute, 2002), 18, 19, 21–2, 66

Alan Kramer, *Dynamic of Destruction: Culture and Mass Killing in the First World War* (Oxford: Oxford University Press, 2007), 65–7, 59–60

Jonas Kreienbaum, '"Vernichtungslager" in Deutsch-Südwestafrika? Zur Funktion der Konzentrationslager im Herero- und Namakrieg (1904–1908)', *Zeitschrift für Geschichtswissenschaft*, 58:12 (2010)

Jonas Kreienbaum, '"Wir sind keine Sklavenhalter": Zur Rolle der Zwangsarbeit in den Konzentrationslagern in Deutsch Südwestafrika (1904 bis 1908)', in Christoph Jahr and Jens Thiel (eds), *Lager vor Auschwitz: Gewalt und Integration im 20. Jahrhundert* (Berlin: Metropol, 2013)

Jonas Kreienbaum, *'Ein trauriges Fiasko': Koloniale Konzentrationslager im südlichen Afrika 1900–1908* (Hamburg: Hamburger Edition, 2015)

Jonas Kreienbaum, 'Deadly Learning? Concentration Camps in Colonial Wars around 1900', in Volker Barth and Roland Cvetkovski (eds), *Imperial Co-operation and Transfer, 1870–1930: Empires and Encounters* (London: Bloomsbury, 2015), 228

A. Dirk Moses, 'An Antipodean Genocide? The Origins of the Genocidal Moment in the Colonization of Australia', *Journal of Genocide Research*, 2:1 (2000)

Klaus Mühlhahn, 'The Concentration Camp in Global Historical Perspective', *History Compass*, 8:6 (2010), 549, 552

Fransjohan Pretorius, 'The White Concentration Camps of the Anglo-Boer War: A Debate without End', *Historia*, 55:2 (2010)

Iain Smith and Andreas Stucki, 'The Development of Concentration Camps', *Journal of Imperial and Commonwealth History*, 39:3 (2011), 418, 419

Ronald Grigor Suny, *'They Can Live in the Desert but Nowhere Else': A History of the Armenian Genocide* (Princeton: Princeton University Press, 2015), 314, 315

Elizabeth Van Heyningen, '"Costly Mythologies": The Concentration Camps of the South African War in Afrikaner Historiography', *Journal of Southern African Studies*, 34:3 (2008)

Elizabeth Van Heyningen, 'The Concentration Camps of the South African (Anglo-Boer) War, 1900–1902', *History Compass*, 7:1 (2009)

Elizabeth Van Heyningen, *The Concentration Camps of the Anglo-Boer War: A Social History* (Auckland Park: Jacana, 2013), 65, 3–4

Jürgen Zimmerer, 'Krieg, KZ und Völkermord im Südwestafrika: Der erste deutsche Genozid'; Joachim Zeller, '"Ombepera i koza—Die Kälte tötet mich": Zur Geschichte des Konzentrationslagers im Swakopmund (1904–1908)'; Casper W. Erichsen, 'Zwangsarbeit im Konzentrationslager auf der Haifischinsel', all in Jürgen Zimmerer and Joachim Zeller (eds), *Völkermord in Deutsch-Südwestafrika: Der Kolonialkrieg (1904–1908) in Namibia und seine Folgen* (Berlin: Christoph Links Verlag, 2003)

Jürgen Zimmerer, *Deutsche Herrschaft über Afrikaner: Staatlicher Machtanspruch und Wirklichkeit im kolonialen Namibia* (Münster: LIT Verlag, 2004), 46

Chapter 3: The Third Reich's world of camps

Jean Ancel, *Transnistria*, vol. 1 (Bucharest: Editura Atlas, 1998)

Hannah Arendt, 'The Concentration Camps', *Partisan Review*, 15:7 (1948), 743

Maurice Blanchot, *The Writing of the Disaster* (Lincoln: University of Nebraska Press, 1986), 82

E. K. Bramstedt, *Dictatorship and Political Police: The Technique of Control by Fear* (London: Routledge, Trench, Trubner and Co., 1945), 133

Marc Buggeln, 'Were Concentration Camp Prisoners Slaves? The Possibilities and Limits of Comparative History and Global History Perspectives', *International Review of Social History*, 53 (2008), 125

Marc Buggeln, *Das System der KZ-Außenlager: Krieg, Sklavenarbeit und Massengewalt* (Bonn: Friedrich-Ebert-Stiftung, 2012)

Richard Dimbleby, 'Despatch of 17 April 1945', in Ben Flanagan and Donald Bloxham (eds), *Remembering Belsen: Eyewitnesses Record the Liberation* (London: Vallentine Mitchell, 2005), xi–xiii

Barbara Distel, 'Die Befreiung des Konzentrationslagers Dachau', *Dachauer Hefte*, 1 (1993), 3

Robert Gellately, *Backing Hitler: Consent and Coercion in Nazi Germany* (Oxford: Oxford University Press, 2001), 204

Christian Goeschel and Nikolaus Wachsmann (eds), *The Nazi Concentration Camps, 1933–1939: A Documentary History* (Lincoln: University of Nebraska Press, 2012), 297

Sebastian Haffner, *Defying Hitler: A Memoir* (London: Phoenix, 2003), 221, 224, 230, 231

Věra Hájková-Duxová, 'Such was Life', in Anita Franková (ed.), *World without Human Dimensions: Four Women's Memories* (Prague: State Jewish Museum, 1991), 101

G. R. Kay, *Dachau: The Nazi Hell: From the Notes of a Former Prisoner at the Notorious Nazi Concentration Camp* (London: Francis Aldor, 1939)

Percy Knauth, *Germany in Defeat* (New York: Alfred A. Knopf, 1946), 32, 42, 62–3

Thomas Kühne, *Belonging and Genocide: Hitler's Community, 1918–1945* (New Haven: Yale University Press, 2010)

Lawrence Langer, *Versions of Survival: The Holocaust and the Human Spirit* (Albany: SUNY Press, 1982)

Stefan Lorant, *I Was Hitler's Prisoner: Leaves from a Prison Diary* (Harmondsworth: Penguin, 1939), 12, 13, 73, 274, 277

Gabriele Lotfi, *KZ der Gestapo: Arbeitserziehungslager im Dritten Reich* (Stuttgart: Deutsche Verlags-Anstalt, 2000)

Samuel Moyn, 'In the Aftermath of Camps', in Frank Biess and Robert G. Moeller (eds), *Histories of the Aftermath: The Legacies of the Second World War in Europe* (New York: Berghahn Books, 2010)

Armin Nolzen, 'Inklusion und Exklusion im "Dritten Reich": Das Beispiel der NSDAP', in Frank Bajohr and Michael Wildt (eds), *Volksgemeinschaft: Neue Forschungen zur Gesellschaft des Nationalsozialismus* (Frankfurt am Main: Fischer Taschenbuch Verlag, 2009)

Boris Pahor, *Necropolis* (Champaign and London: Dalkey Archive Press, 2010), 131

Kiran Klaus Patel, *Soldiers of Labor: Labor Service in Nazi Germany and New Deal America, 1933–1945* (Cambridge: Cambridge University Press, 2005)

Kiran Klaus Patel, 'Volksgenossen und Gemeinschaftsfremde: Über den Doppelcharakter der nationalsozialistischen Lager', in Christoph Jahr and Jens Thiel (eds), *Lager vor Auschwitz: Gewalt und Integration im 20. Jahrhundert* (Berlin: Metropol, 2013)

Anna Pawełczyńska, *Values and Violence in Auschwitz: A Sociological Analysis* (Berkeley: University of California Press, 1980)

Anson Rabinbach and Sander L. Gilman (eds), *The Third Reich Sourcebook* (Berkeley: University of California Press, 2013), 223

Maximilian Reich, 'Mörder-Schule: Konzentrationslager', Wiener Library P.III.h.No. 1058 (Dachau), 3

Isaac Rosenfeld, 'Terror beyond Evil', *New Leader*, 31:7 (14 February 1948), reprinted in *Preserving the Hunger: An Isaac Rosenfeld Reader*, ed. Mark Shechner (Detroit: Wayne State University Press, 1988), 129–30

Ion Şerbanescu et al. (eds), *Evreii din România între anii 1940–1944*, vol. 3: *1940–1942: Perioada unei mari restrişti. Partea a II-a* (Bucharest: Hasefer, 1997)

Wolfgang Sofsky, *The Order of Terror: The Concentration Camp* (Princeton: Princeton University Press, 1997)

Dan Stone, *Responses to Nazism in Britain, 1933–1939: Before War and Holocaust*, 2nd edn (Houndmills: Palgrave Macmillan, 2012)

Maja Suderland, *Inside Concentration Camps: Social Life at the Extremes* (Cambridge: Polity Press, 2013)

Nikolaus Wachsmann, *KL: A History of the Nazi Concentration Camps* (London: Little, Brown, 2015), 489

References

G. Ward Price, *I Know These Dictators* (London: George G. Harrap & Co., 1937), 119

Michael Wildt, 'Funktionswandel der nationalsozialistische Lager', *Mittelweg 36*, 20:4 (2011), 80

Edith Wyschogrod, *Spirit in Ashes: Hegel, Heidegger, and Man-Made Mass Death* (New Haven: Yale University Press, 1985)

Joop Zwart, 'The Last Days of Bergen-Belsen', Wiener Library P. III.h.No.780 (Bergen-Belsen), 10

Chapter 4: The Gulag

Nanci Adler, 'The Return of the Repressed: Survival after the Gulag', in Daniel Bertaux, Paul Thompson, and Anna Rotkirch (eds), *On Living through Soviet Russia* (London: Routledge, 2004)

Golfo Alexopoulos, 'Amnesty 1945: The Revolving Door of Stalin's Gulag', *Slavic Review*, 64:2 (2005), 275

Alan Barenberg, 'Prisoners without Borders: Zazonniki and the Transformation of Vorkuta after Stalin', *Jahrbücher für Geschichte Osteuropas*, 57:4 (2009), 515, 517, 529

Alan Barenberg, *Gulag Town, Company Town: Forced Labor and its Legacy in Vorkuta* (New Haven: Yale University Press, 2014), 29, 35, 86, 11

Steven A. Barnes, *Death and Redemption: The Gulag and the Shaping of Soviet Society* (Princeton: Princeton University Press, 2011), 2, 12, 15

Wilson T. Bell, 'Was the Gulag an Archipelago? De-convoyed Prisoners and Porous Borders in the Camps of Western Siberia', *Russian Review*, 72 (2013), 130, 139

Kate Brown, 'Out of Solitary Confinement: The History of the Gulag', *Kritika*, 8:1 (2007), 102

Richard Evans, 'The Anatomy of Hell', *New York Review of Books* (9 July 2015)

Cathy A. Frierson and Semyon S. Vilensky, *Children of the Gulag* (New Haven: Yale University Press, 2010), 104, 294

Jehanne M. Gheith and Katherine R. Jolluck, *Gulag Voices: Oral Histories of Soviet Incarceration and Exile* (New York: Palgrave Macmillan, 2011), 24

Małgorzata Giżejewska, 'Die Einzigartigkeit und der besondere Charakter der Konzentrationslager in Kolyma und die Möglichkeiten des Überlebens', in Dittmar Dahlmann and Gerhard Hirschfeld (eds), *Lager, Zwangsarbeit, Vertreibung und*

Deportation: Dimensionen der Massenverbrechen in der Sowjetunion und in Deutschland 1933–1945 (Essen: Klartext, 1999)

Paul R. Gregory and Valery Lazarev (eds), *The Economics of Forced Labor: The Soviet Gulag* (Washington, DC: Hoover Institution, 2003)

Gustaw Herling, *A World Apart* (New York: Penguin, 1996), 175–6

Galina Mikhailovna Ivanova, *Labor Camp Socialism: The Gulag in the Soviet Totalitarian System* (London: Routledge, 2015), 185, 188

Oleg V. Khlevniuk, *The History of the Gulag: From Collectivization to the Great Terror* (New Haven: Yale University Press, 2004), 178, 113

Oleg Khlevniuk, 'Comments on the Short-Term Consequences of the Holodomor', in Andrea Graziosi, Lubomyr A. Hajda, and Halyna Hryn (eds), *After the Holodomor: The Enduring Impact of the Great Famine on Ukraine* (Cambridge, MA: Harvard University Press, 2013), 157

Oxana Klimkova, 'Special Settlements in Soviet Russia in the 1930s–50s', *Kritika*, 8:1 (2007), 128

S. A. Malsagoff, *An Island Hell: A Soviet Prison in the Far North* (London: A. M. Philpot, 1926)

Fyodor Vasilevich Mochulsky, *Gulag Boss: A Soviet Memoir*, ed. Deborah Kaple (New York: Oxford University Press, 2011), 107, 168–9

David J. Nordlander, 'Origins of a Gulag Capital: Magadan and Stalinist Control in the Early 1930s', *Slavic Review*, 57:4 (1998), 793

David J. Nordlander, 'Magadan and the Evolution of the Dal'stroi Bosses in the 1930s', *Cahiers du monde russe*, 42:2–4 (2001), 649

Judith Pallot, 'Russia's Penal Peripheries: Space, Place and Penalty in Soviet and Post-Soviet Russia', *Transactions of the Institute of British Geographers*, 30:1 (2005), 100

Felix Schnell, 'Der Gulag als Systemstelle sowjetischer Herrschaft', in Bettina Greiner and Alan Kramer (eds), *Welt der Lager: Zur 'Erfolgsgeschichte' einer Institution* (Hamburg: Hamburger Edition, 2013), 134, 161

Jorge Semprun, *What a Beautiful Sunday!* (London: Abacus, 1984), 104

Avraham Shifrin, *The First Guidebook to Prisons and Concentration Camps of the Soviet Union* (Toronto: Bantam Books, 1982), 31

Andrei Sokolov, 'Forced Labor in the Soviet Union: The End of the 1930s to the Mid-1950s', in Paul R. Gregory and Valery Lazarev (eds), *The Economics of Forced Labor: The Soviet Gulag* (Washington, DC: Hoover Institution Press, 2003), 39–40

Alexander Solzhenitsyn, *The Gulag Archipelago 1918–1956* (London: Collins Harvill, 1988), 256

Tzvetan Todorov, *Hope and Memory: Reflections on the Twentieth Century* (London: Atlantic Books, 2005), 105

Nicolas Werth, *Cannibal Island: Death in a Siberian Gulag* (Princeton: Princeton University Press, 2007)

Nicolas Werth, 'The Crimes of the Stalin Regime: Outline for an Inventory and Classification', in Dan Stone (ed.), *The Historiography of Genocide* (Houndmills: Palgrave Macmillan, 2008), 404

Nicolas Werth, 'Mass Deportations, Ethnic Cleansing, and Genocidal Politics in the Later Russian Empire and the USSR', in Donald Bloxham and A. Dirk Moses (eds), *The Oxford Handbook of Genocide Studies* (Oxford: Oxford University Press, 2010)

Chapter 5: The wide world of camps

David Anderson, *Histories of the Hanged: Britain's Dirty War in Kenya and the End of Empire* (London: Weidenfeld and Nicolson, 2004), 313, 315

Kang Chol-hwan and Pierre Rigoulot, *The Aquariums of Pyongyang: Ten Years in a North Korean Gulag* (Oxford: Perseus Press, 2001), 40, 160

Commission internationale contre le régime concentrationnaire (CICRC), *Livre blanc sur le système pénitentiaire espagnol* (Paris: Le Pavois, 1953), 23

Stéphane Courtois et al., *The Black Book of Communism: Crimes, Terror, Repression* (Cambridge, MA: Harvard University Press, 1999)

Adriano Dal Pont, *I lager di Mussolini: l'altra faccia del confine nei documenti della polizia fascista* (Milan: La Pietra, 1975)

Roger Daniels, *Concentration Camps USA: Japanese Americans and World War II* (New York: Holt, Rinehart and Winston, 1971), 45–6, 72, 142–3

Roger Daniels, 'The Decision for Mass Evacuation', in Alice Yang Murray (ed.), *What Did the Internment of Japanese Americans Mean?* (Boston: Bedford/St Martin's, 2000), 58

Roger Daniels, *Prisoners without Trial: Japanese Americans in World War II*, rev. edn (New York: Hill and Wang, 2004)

Michael R. Ebner, *Ordinary Violence in Mussolini's Italy* (New York: Cambridge University Press, 2011), 104, 127, 138

Caroline Elkins, *Britain's Gulag: The Brutal End of Empire in Kenya* (London: Jonathan Cape, 2004), 121, 155, 153, 188

Moritz Feichtinger, '"Concentration Camps in all but Name"? Zwangsumsiedlung und Counterinsurgency, 1950–1970', in Bettina Greiner and Alan Kramer (eds), *Welt der Lager: Zur 'Erfolgsgeschichte' einer Institution* (Hamburg: Hamburger Edition, 2013), 311, 303

Christian Gerlach, *Extremely Violent Societies: Mass Violence in the Twentieth-Century World* (New York: Cambridge University Press, 2010), 191

Helen Graham, *The War and its Shadow: Spain's Civil War in Europe's Long Twentieth Century* (Brighton: Sussex Academic Press, 2012), 18, 110, 112, 103

Anne Grynberg, *Les camps de la honte: les internés juifs des camps français 1939–1944* (Paris: Editions La Découverte, 1991)

Earl G. Harrison, letter accompanying the Harrison Report, https://www.ushmm.org/exhibition/displaced-persons/resourc1.htm

Ira A. Hirschman, *The Embers Still Burn: An Eye-witness View of the Postwar Ferment in Europe and the Middle East and Our Disastrous Get-soft-with Germany Policy* (New York: Simon and Schuster, 1949), 34

Virgil Ierunca, *Fenomenul Pitești* (Bucharest: Humanitas, 2013)

Tetsuden Kashima, *Judgment without Trial: Japanese American Imprisonment during World War II* (Seattle: University of Washington Press, 2003), 8

Arthur Koestler, *Scum of the Earth* (London: Eland, 2006 [1941]), 93, 94

Joël Kotek and Pierre Rigoulot, *Le siècle des camps: détention, concentration, extermination: cent ans de mal radical* (Paris: J. C. Lattès, 2000), 567

François Lafitte, *The Internment of Aliens* (Harmondsworth: Penguin, 1940), 27

Fernando Mendiola Gonzalo, 'Forced Labor, Public Policies, and Business Strategies during Franco's Dictatorship: An Interim Report', *Enterprise and Society*, 14:1 (2013), 188

Carme Molinero et al. (eds), *Una imensa prisión: los campos de concentración y las prisiones durante la guerra civil y el franquismo* (Barcelona: Crítica, 2003)

Klaus Mühlhahn, 'The Dark Side of Globalization: The Concentration Camps in Republican China in Global Perspective', *World History Connected*, 6:1 (2009)

Miné Okubo, *Citizen 13660* (New York: Columbia University Press, 1946), 61, 81

Taylor Owen and Ben Kiernan, 'Bombs over Cambodia', *The Walrus* (October 2006), 63

Rithy Panh with Christophe Bataille, *The Elimination: A Survivor of the Khmer Rouge Confronts His Past and the Commandant of the Killing Fields* (London: The Clerkenwell Press, 2013), 259

Paul Preston, *The Spanish Holocaust: Inquisition and Extermination in Twentieth-Century Spain* (London: HarperCollins, 2012)

Luigi Reale, *Mussolini's Concentration Camps for Civilians: An Insight into the Nature of Fascist Racism* (London: Vallentine Mitchell, 2011), 1, 61, 114

Javier Rodrigo, 'Exploitation, Fascist Violence and Social Cleansing: A Study of Franco's Concentration Camps from a Comparative Perspective', *European Review of History*, 19:4 (2012), 559, 557

Javier Rodrigo, 'Der Faschismus und die Lager in Spanien und Italien', in Bettina Greiner and Alan Kramer (eds), *Welt der Lager: Zur 'Erfolgsgeschichte' einer Institution* (Hamburg: Hamburger Edition, 2013)

Simon Schochet, *Feldafing* (Vancouver: November House, 1983)

Michael Seyfert, '"His Majesty's Most Loyal Internees"', in Gerhard Hirschfeld (ed.), *Exile in Great Britain: Refugees from Hitler's Germany* (Leamington Spa: Berg, 1984), 180

Mircea Stănescu, *Reeducarea în România comunistă (1945–1952): Aiud, Suceava, Pitești, Brașov* (Iași: Polirom, 2010)

Dan Stone, *The Liberation of the Camps: The End and Aftermath of the Holocaust* (New Haven: Yale University Press, 2015)

Philip F. Williams and Yenna Wu, *The Great Wall of Confinement: The Chinese Prison Camp through Contemporary Fiction and Reportage* (Berkeley: University of California Press, 2004), 2, 5

Hongda Harry Wu, *Laogai: The Chinese Gulag* (Boulder: Westview Press, 1992), 5, 15, 34

Harry Wu and Carolyn Wakeman, *Bitter Winds: A Memoir of My Years in China's Gulag* (New York: John Wiley & Sons, 1994), 283

Chapter 6: 'An Auschwitz every three months': society as camp?

Giorgio Agamben, *Homo Sacer: Sovereign Power and Bare Life* (Stanford: Stanford University Press, 1998), 166, 168–9

Hannah Arendt, *The Origins of Totalitarianism*, rev. edn (San Diego: Harcourt Brace & Company, 1979), 447

Zygmunt Bauman, 'A Century of Camps?', in *The Bauman Reader*, ed. Peter Beilharz (Oxford: Blackwell, 2001), 274–5

Christian Gerlach, *Extremely Violent Societies: Mass Violence in the Twentieth-Century World* (New York: Cambridge University Press, 2010), 183

Paolo Giaccaria and Claudio Minca, 'Topographies/Topologies of the Camp: Auschwitz as a Spatial Threshold', *Political Geography*, 30 (2011)

Ruth Wilson Gilmore, *Golden Gulag: Prisons, Surplus, Crisis, and Opposition in Globalizing California* (Berkeley: University of California Press, 2007)

Eugenia Ginzburg, *Into the Whirlwind* (London: Collins Harvill, 1989), 80

Erving Goffman, *Asylums: Essays on the Social Situation of Mental Patients and Other Inmates* (Harmondsworth: Penguin, 1968)

Alona Gordeew, *'Archipele' des Ausnahmezustands: Konzentrationslager im Dritten Reich und der Gulag in der früheren Sowjetunion* (Norderstedt: Grin Verlag, 2010)

Galina Mikhailovna Ivanova, *Labor Camp Socialism: The Gulag in the Soviet Totalitarian System* (London: Routledge, 2015), 191

Vinay Lal, 'The Concentration Camp and Development: The Pasts and Future of Genocide', *Patterns of Prejudice*, 39:2 (2005), 241

Alphonso Lingis, *Abuses* (Berkeley: University of California Press, 1994), 36

Alan Moorehead, *Eclipse* (London: Hamish Hamilton, 1945), 229

Richard Overy, 'The Concentration Camp: An International Perspective', *Eurozine* (2011), online at: http://www.eurozine.com/articles/2011-08-25-overy-en.html

Boris Pahor, *Necropolis* (Champaign and London: Dalkey Archive Press, 2010), 83

Bertrand Perz, 'Lager im 20. Jahrhundert', *H-Soz-Kult* (22 May 2014)

Javier Rodrigo, 'Exploitation, Fascist Violence and Social Cleansing: A Study of Franco's Concentration Camps from a Comparative Perspective', *European Review of History*, 19:4 (2012), 562, 563

Isaac Rosenfeld, 'The Meaning of Terror' (1949), in *Preserving the Hunger: An Isaac Rosenfeld Reader*, ed. Mark Shechner (Detroit: Wayne State University Press, 1988), 133

Rainer Schulze, 'Immediate Images: British Narratives of the Liberation of Bergen-Belsen', in Habbo Knoch and Thomas Rahe (eds), *Bergen-Belsen: Neue Forschungen* (Göttingen: Wallstein, 2014), 279

Jörg Später, 'Jahrhundert der Lager? Über Stärken und Schwächen eines Begriffs', *iz3w*, 239 (1999)

Ichiro Takayoshi, 'Can Philosophy Explain Nazi Violence? Giorgio Agamben and the Problem of the "Historico-Philosophical" Method', *Journal of Genocide Research*, 13:1–2 (2011), 55

Further reading

Chapter 1: What is a concentration camp?

On Hannah Arendt, see Richard H. King and Dan Stone (eds), *Hannah Arendt and the Uses of History* (New York: Berghahn Books, 2007) and Richard H. King, *Arendt and America* (Chicago: University of Chicago Press, 2015). Arendt's essays 'Social Science Techniques and the Study of Concentration Camps', in Arendt, *Essays in Understanding, 1930–1954*, ed. Jerome H. Kohn (New York: Harcourt Brace & Company, 1994), and 'Concentration Camps', *Partisan Review*, 15:7 (1948), 743–63, remain thought-provoking texts. On 'licence', see Aristotle Kallis, *Genocide and Fascism: The Eliminationist Drive in Fascist Europe* (London: Routledge, 2009). Patrick Gordon Walker's book can usefully be compared with Derrick Sington, *Belsen Uncovered* (London: Duckworth, 1946).

Chapter 2: Origins

On the origins of camps, see Bettina Greiner and Alan Kramer (eds), *Die Welt der Lager: Zur 'Erfolgsgeschichte' einer Institution* (Hamburg: Hamburger Edition, 2013); Christoph Jahr and Jens Thiel (eds), *Lager vor Auschwitz: Gewalt und Integration im 20. Jahrhundert* (Berlin: Metropol Verlag, 2013); and Joël Kotek and Pierre Rigoulet, *Le siècle des camps: détention, concentration, extermination: cent ans de mal radical* (Paris: J. C. Lattès, 2000). For a thoughtful analysis of concentration camps in the British Empire and their connections with camps in the 20th century, see Aidan Forth, *Barbed-Wire Imperialism: Britain's Empire of Camps, 1876–1903* (Oakland: University of California Press, 2017). Excellent general overviews are provided by Richard Overy, 'The Concentration Camp: An International Perspective', *Eurozine* (2011, online) and Klaus Mühlhahn, 'The Concentration Camp in Global Historical Perspective', *History Compass*, 8:6 (2010), 543–61. Other useful surveys are Andrzej J. Kaminski, *Konzentrationslager 1896 bis heute: Geschichte, Funktion, Typologie* (Munich: Piper, 1990); Hermann Scharnagl, *Kurze Geschichte der Konzentrationslager* (Wiesbaden: Marix Verlag, 2004); and Wolfgang Wippermann, *Konzentrationslager: Geschichte, Nachgeschichte, Gedenken* (Berlin: Elefanten Press, 1999).

Chapter 3: The Third Reich's world of camps

The single best volume on the Nazi camps is Nikolaus Wachsmann, *KL: A History of the Nazi Concentration Camps* (London: Little, Brown, 2015). See also his chapter, 'The Nazi Concentration Camps in International Context: Comparisons and Connections', in Jan Rüger and Nikolaus Wachsmann (eds), *Rewriting German History: New Perspectives on Modern Germany* (Houndmills: Palgrave Macmillan, 2015). Among the vast literature, some recent works have clarified the ways in which the different camps and camp system overall developed over time. See, for example, Jane Caplan and Nikolaus Wachsmann (eds), *Concentration Camps in Nazi Germany: The New Histories* (Abingdon: Routledge, 2010); Kim Wünschmann, *Before Auschwitz: Jewish Prisoners in the Prewar Concentration Camps* (Cambridge, MA: Harvard University Press, 2015); Christopher Dillon, *Dachau and the SS: A Schooling in Violence* (Oxford: Oxford University Press, 2015). On slave labour see Marc Buggeln, *Slave Labor in Nazi Concentration Camps* (Oxford: Oxford University Press, 2014) and Michael Thad Allen, *The Business of Genocide: The SS, Slave Labor, and the Concentration Camps* (Chapel Hill: University of North Carolina Press, 2002). And for overviews, see also Karin Orth, *Das System der nationalsozialistischen Konzentrationslager* (Zurich: Pendo, 2002) and Ulrich Herbert et al. (eds), *Die nationalsozialistischen Konzentrationslager*, 2 vols (Frankfurt am Main: Fischer Taschenbuch Verlag, 2002); Wolfgang Benz et al.'s multi-volume series *Geschichte der Konzentrationslager 1933–1945*

(Berlin: Metropol); Geoffrey Megargee (ed.), *Encyclopedia of Camps and Ghettos* (United States Holocaust Memorial Museum), and for a recent sociological study, Maja Suderland, *Inside Concentration Camps: Social Life at the Extremes* (Cambridge: Polity Press, 2013). Good studies of individual camps include: Gordon J. Horwitz, *In the Shadow of Death: Living Outside the Gates of Mauthausen* (New York: The Free Press, 1990); Bella Gutterman, *A Narrow Bridge to Life: Jewish Forced Labor in the Gross-Rosen Camp System, 1940–1945* (New York: Berghahn Books, 2008); Habbo Knoch and Thomas Rahe (eds), *Bergen-Belsen: Neue Forschungen* (Göttingen: Wallstein, 2014).

Chapter 4: The Gulag

Alexander Solzhenitsyn's *The Gulag Archipelago* is still the essential starting point. That said, the scholarly literature has developed a great deal since Cold War days and there is now a mature historiography. In addition to texts mentioned in the References section, this includes: Michael Jakobson, *Origins of the Gulag: The Soviet Prison Camp System 1917–1934* (Lexington: University Press of Kentucky, 1993) and Lynne Viola, *The Unknown Gulag: The Lost World of Stalin's Special Settlements* (New York: Oxford University Press, 2007). A useful historiographical overview is Wilson T. Bell, 'Gulag Historiography: An Introduction', *Gulag Studies*, 2–3 (2009–10). Testimonies are also now more widely available in English, including in: Leona Toker, *Return from the Archipelago: Narratives of Gulag Survivors* (Bloomington: Indiana University Press, 2000) and Stephen F. Cohen, *The Victims Return: Survivors of the Gulag after Stalin* (London: I. B. Tauris, 2012). Major literary works include Varlam Shalamov, *Kolyma Tales* (New York: W. W. Norton, 1982); Gustaw Herling, *A World Apart* (New York: Penguin, 1996); Eugenia Ginzburg, *Into the Whirlwind* (London: Collins Harvill, 1989); and the remarkable Margarete Buber-Neumann, *Under Two Dictators: Prisoner of Hitler and Stalin* (London: Pimlico, 2008). Useful comparative studies include: Gerhard Armanski, *Maschinen des Terrors: Das Lager (KZ und GULAG) in der Moderne* (Münster: Westfälisches Dampfboot, 1993) and Ian Kershaw and Moshe Lewin (eds), *Stalinism and Nazism: Dictatorships in Comparison* (Cambridge: Cambridge University Press, 1997).

Chapter 5: The wide world of camps

The following texts are recommended as supplements to the literature cited in the text: Atina Grossmann, *Jews, Germans and Allies: Close Encounters in Occupied Germany* (Princeton: Princeton University Press, 2007); Margarete Myers Feinstein, *Holocaust Survivors in Postwar Germany, 1945–1957* (New York: Cambridge University Press, 2010); Kate Saunders, *Eighteen Layers of Hell: Stories from the Chinese Gulag* (London: Cassell, 1996); Frank Dikötter, *Mao's Great Famine* (London: Bloomsbury, 2010). Many of these texts are discussed in Gregory Claeys, *Dystopia: A Natural History* (Oxford: Oxford University Press, 2017).

Chapter 6: 'An Auschwitz every three months': society as camp?

Apart from the texts listed in the References section, on the meaning of the camps for modernity, see also: Zygmunt Bauman, *Modernity and the Holocaust* (Cambridge: Polity Press, 1989); Michel Foucault, *Society Must Be Defended: Lectures at the Collège de France 1975–1976* (London: Allen Lane, 2003); Anne Kelly Knowles, Tim Cole, and Albert Giordano (eds), *Geographies of the Holocaust* (Bloomington: Indiana University Press, 2014); Paolo Giaccaria and Claudio Minca (eds), *Hitler's Geographies: The Spatialities of the Third Reich* (Chicago: University of Chicago Press, 2016); Griselda Pollock and Max Silverman (eds), *Concentrationary Memories: Totalitarian Terror and Cultural Resistance* (London: I. B. Tauris, 2013); and Griselda Pollock and Max Silverman (eds), *Concentrationary Imaginaries: Tracing Totalitarian Terror in Popular Culture* (London: I. B. Tauris, 2015). On refugee camps, see Nando Sigona, 'Campzenship: Reimagining the Camp as a Social and Political Space', *Journal of Citizenship Studies*, 19:1 (2015), 1–15, and Jordanna Bailkin, *Unsettled: Refugee Camps and the Making of Multicultural Britain* (Oxford: Oxford University Press, 2018). And on the idea of 'society as camp', see Bülent Diken and Carsten Bagge Laustsen, *The Culture of Exception: Sociology Facing the Camp* (Abingdon: Routledge, 2005), and Colman Hogan and Marta Marin-Dòmine (eds), *The Camp: Narratives of Internment and Exclusion* (Newcastle: Cambridge Scholars, 2007).

Publisher's Acknowledgements

We are grateful for permission to include the following copyright material in this book:

Excerpt from *The Origins of Totalitarianism*, by Hannah Arendt. Copyright 1951 by Hannah Arendt. Copyright © renewed 1979 by Mary McCarthy West. Reprinted by permission of Houghton Mifflin Publishing Company. All rights reserved.

The publisher and author have made every effort to trace and contact all copyright holders before publication. If notified, the publisher will be pleased to rectify any errors or omissions at the earliest opportunity.

Index

A

Adriatisches Küstenland 73
Adzhimambetova,
    Adzhigulsum 62
Africa 2, 69, 74
Agamben, Giorgio 2, 6, 96–8,
    100, 101
Aguinaldo, Emilio 13
Aguthi (Kenya) 86
Akçam, Taner 26
Albania 73
Alexopoulos, Golfo 52
Algeria 2, 22, 71, 85, 99, 103
Algerian War 87
    camps de regroupement in 87
Aliens Restriction Act (Britain,
    1914) 23
American Indians 11–12
Anderson, David 85
Anglo-American Committee
    of Inquiry on Palestine
    (1946) 81
Anglo-Boer War 6, 9, 10, 13, 14–17,
    15, 16, 27, 32, 37
    Afrikaner memory of 14, 15
    black Africans in 14–15

Arendt, Hannah 7–9, 34, 35, 36,
    37, 67, 74, 94, 101, 103,
    105, 106
Argelès (France) 74
Argentina 48, 70, 92
Armenian genocide 2, 23,
    25–7, 37
Auschwitz 4, 35, 39, 40, 42, 51, 52,
    57, 68, 73, 99, 104, 106, 109,
    110, 112
Australia 2, 12
    see also Tasmania
Austria 22, 80, 81, 109
Averianov, Nikolai 50–1

B

Balashina, Sira Stepanovna 66
Baltic States 83
Bangladesh 114
Barenberg, Alan 59
Barnes, Steven 65, 67, 68
Bauman, Zygmunt 2–3, 100–2,
    103, 106
Bela (Czech Republic) 98
Belgium 22
Bell, Wilson 58–9, 61, 68

Belsen 9, 33, 35, 40, 43, 46–7, 81, 82, 108–9, 111, 112, 113
Bełżec 4, 40
Beria, Lavrenty 64
Berzin, Eduard Petrovich 55
Bettelheim, Bruno 34
Bevin, Ernest 82
Blanchot, Maurice 36
Böll, Uwe 110
Bosnia 3, 92, 103, 112
Bourdieu, Pierre 102
Bramstedt, E. K. 34
Britain 6, 10, 12, 14, 15, 16, 17, 69, 87–8
  internment of 'enemy aliens' 76, 79–80
  and Mau Mau Uprising 85–7, 86
British Army Film and Photographic Unit 108–9
British East Africa 23
Brown, Dave 95
Brown, Kate 66
Buber-Neumann, Margarete 53
Buchenwald 6, 33, 35, 37–8, 39, 40, 43, 47, 48, 52, 70, 83, 84, 109
Buggeln, Marc 42
Bund Deutscher Mädel 44

C

Cambodia 2, 88, 89–90, 112
Cameroon 22
Canada 79
Celan, Paul 110
Chacabuco (Chile) 110
Chapman Brothers 110
Chechens 62–3
Chełmno 4, 40
Chile 70, 92, 95
China 2, 6, 7, 28, 29, 71, 88
  Cultural Revolution 111
  Great Leap Forward 111
  laogai system in 90–2

Choeung Ek (Cambodia) 90
Chol-hwan, Kang 92
Christianstadt (sub-camp of Gross-Rosen) 42, 110–11, 111
Chukotka (Soviet Union) 53
Cold War 58, 64, 76, 79, 81
Colnbrook detention centre (UK) 98
colonialism 8, 10, 11, 13, 15, 17, 18, 20, 24, 83, 84–5, 88, 100, 102–3
Commission internationale contre le régime concentrationnaire (CICRC) 70–1, 75
communist countries' camps 88–92
Cuba 2, 10, 11, 13, 14, 15, 17, 19, 49, 96, 99
  Spanish–American War 13
Cyprus, Jewish DP camps in 2, 69, 82–3, 85, 112

D

Dachau 6, 9, 10, 30–1, 32, 33, 35, 37, 38, 40, 43, 49, 65, 67, 74–5, 78, 82, 83, 84, 94, 98, 112–13
Daderian, Vahram 25
Dahomey 22
Daily Mail 31
Dal'stroi (Soviet Union) 55
Daniels, Roger 77, 79
'death marches' 43
decolonization 2
de Gaulle, Charles 87
Democratic Republic of Congo 9
Der el Zor (Ottoman Empire) 26–7
development 98–9
De Witt, John L. 76–7
Diestel, Peter-Michael 84
Dimbleby, Richard 47
Displaced Persons (DPs) 2, 3, 69, 80–3, 112

Distel, Barbara 43
Dmitlag (Soviet Union) 59
Domenach, Jean-Luc 90
Dr Seuss (Theodor Geisel) 77

E

Ebensee (sub-camp of
     Mauthausen) 35
Ebner, Michael 72
Egypt 48
Eicke, Theodor 38, 76
Elkins, Caroline 86
Enlightenment 101
Esterwegen 84
'Euthanasia Programme' (Nazi
     Germany) 4
Evans, Richard 52

F

fascism 7, 8, 71, 72, 73, 76, 80
favelas 3
Feichtinger, Moritz 88
Ferenc, Tone 72–3
Fink, Ida 110
First World War 20–4, 28, 29,
     37, 108
Flossenbürg 84
Foucault, Michel 96
France 6, 20, 22, 24, 69, 70, 73–5,
     87, 88, 104, 110
   internment of Spanish Civil War
     fighters in 37, 73–5
Franco, Francisco 2, 75, 76,
     103, 110
Frenkel, Naftali 54

G

Gasr Bu Hadi (Libya) 73
Gaza 104–5, 114
Gellately, Robert 39
Geneva Convention (1929) 24
Gerlach, Christian 87, 99

*German Concentration Camps
     Factual Survey* 109
German South-West Africa 2,
     17–19, 18, 27, 28, 37, 49
Germany 22, 27, 80, 81, 83–4,
     111, 112
   Soviet 'special camps' in 70,
     83–4
   Weimar constitution 97
   see also Nazi Germany
Gheith, Jehanne M. 66
Ginzburg, Eugenia 56–7, 59, 104
global south 3, 99–100, 114
Goethe, Johann Wolfgang von 38
Goffman, Erving 102
Gomez, Maximo 13
Gorbachev, Mikhail 65
Gordon Walker, Patrick 4–7
Graham, Helen 75, 76
Greece 48, 71, 98
Gross-Rosen 40, 41, 42
Guantánamo Bay 3, 79, 97, 104,
     105, 106, 112, 114
Gulag 2, 6, 7, 8, 9, 16, 49, 50–68,
     76, 88, 101–2, 103, 105, 106,
     110, 112
   blat in 61
   compared with Nazi camps 51–3,
     61, 65, 67, 68
   definition of 51
   deportation of 'suspect nations'
     to 62–3, 64
   'dezoned' prisoners 58–9, 60
   'Golden' 95
   'Great Terror' and 55, 61, 63
   Kenyan 85
   map 52
   origins of 52–3
   Second World War and 62–3
   'small zone' and 'large zone' 58,
     60, 61, 67
   use of term 95–6
   see also 'special settlements'
Guomindang 28
Gurs (France) 74, 75

H

Haffner, Sebastian 44–5, 46
Hague Convention (1907) 21
Hague Laws (1899) 13
Hájková-Duxová, Věra 42
Harrison, Earl 81
Herero and Nama War (1904–7) 17–19, 18, 27, 28
Herling, Gustaw 57, 68
Herzogenbusch 40
Hierl, Konstantin 44
Himmler, Heinrich 35, 38, 76
Hirschmann, Ira 82
Hitler, Adolf 30, 52–3, 68, 82, 109
Hitler Youth 44
Hobhouse, Emily 14, 16
Holocaust 1, 4, 35, 36, 36–7, 40, 43, 51, 68, 80, 103, 110, 112, 113
Holocaust Memorial Day 112
Hoover, Calvin B. 31
Hull, Isabel 19
Human Rights Watch 94–5
Hungary 95
Hyslop, Jonathan 16, 19, 28–9

I

Imperial War Museum (London) 109
India 6, 23, 48, 113
Indigirka (Soviet Union) 53
internally displaced persons (IDPs) 3, 98
Isle of Man 24, 79
Israel 81, 95, 105
Italy 22, 69, 71–3, 81, 104
  race laws 72
Ivanova, Galina 61

J

Japan 27, 29, 69
  Special Unit 731 (Manchuria) 27

Japanese-Americans, detention of 2, 70, 76–9
  compared with Nazi camps 78
Jasenovac (Croatia) 69
Jaspers, Karl 36, 107
Jehovah's Witnesses 38
Jews 2, 4, 7, 24, 27, 36, 39, 40, 42, 44, 69, 72, 76, 79, 80–3, 112, 113
Jolluck, Katherine R. 66
Jones, Heather 24–5
Jordan 94
'Jungle' (France) 98

K

Kagombe, Nderi 86
Kaing Guek Eav ('Comrade Duch') 90
Kaiser, Hilmar 25, 26
Kantor, Tadeusz 110
Karaganda (Soviet Union) 56
Kashima, Tetsuden 78
Katma (Ghatma) 25–6
Kenya 2, 85–7, 86, 87, 99, 103, 112
  'Pipeline' in 86
  'villagization' 87, 99
  see also Mau Mau uprising
Khlevniuk, Oleg 57, 68
Khmer Rouge 2, 89–90, 112
Khrushchev, Nikita 64
Kitchener, H. H. 16, 29
Knauth, Percy 47–8
Koestler, Arthur 69, 74–5
Kogon, Eugen 34, 37
Kolnai, Aurel 31
Kolyma 53, 54–5, 65
Kotek, Joël 88
'Kristallnacht' 39

L

Lafitte, François 79–80
La Guardia, Fiorello 82

Lal, Vinay 99, 100
Lampedusa 71
Langer, Lawrence 34
Lebanon 94
Le Barcarès (France) 74
Le Vernet (France) 74–5
Levi, Primo 106
Li, Dai 28
Libya 73, 94–5
Lichtenburg 37
Lingis, Alphonso 99–100
Lipari (Italy) 71, 72
Lorant, Stefan 30–1, 32
Low, David 74
Luo Ruiqing 91
Lyttleton, Oliver 85

M

MacArthur, Arthur 13
Magadan 54–5, 59
Magda (sub-camp of
    Buchenwald) 39
Mahon 10
Majdanek 4, 39, 40, 82
Malaya 2, 87, 99, 103, 112
Manzanar (USA) 78
Maschmann, Melita 45–6
Mau Mau uprising
    85–7, 86
Mauthausen 21, 40
Memorial (Russia) 50
Milner, Alfred 16
Mineo (Italy) 98
Minidoka (USA) 78
Miranda de Ebro (Spain) 76
Mittelbau-Dora 39
Mochulsky, Fyodor Vasilevich 57,
    60, 66
Montenegro 93
Moorehead, Alan 111, 112–13
Morocco 22
Mühlhahn, Klaus 24
Musmanno, Michael 1
Mussolini, Benito 72

N

Namibia 110
    see also German
        South-West Africa
Nazi Germany 1, 2, 3, 4, 5, 6–7, 8,
    9, 10, 11, 16, 17, 29, 30–49, 69,
    70, 71, 97, 101, 103, 110, 112, 113
    Labour Service in 44–6
Nazino (Soviet Union) 57
Neuengamme (Germany) 40,
    42, 84
Neumann, Franz 31
Night and Fog 34
NKVD 51, 53, 55, 61
Nordlander, David 55, 67
Nor'ilsk (Soviet Union) 56
North Korea 3, 92, 112
Novosibirsk 58
Nuremberg Trials 1, 36

O

OGPU 51, 54
Okubo, Miné 77–8
Omarska (Bosnia) 92, 111
Operation Anvil (Kenya) 85
Oranienburg (Germany) 37
Ottoman Empire 2, 23, 25, 49
Ouzounian, Naomie 26
Overy, Richard 108

P

Pagis, Dan 110
Pahor, Boris 30, 113–14
Palestine 2, 48, 81, 82, 105, 112
Pallot, Judith 65–6
Pantelleria (Italy) 71
Passmore, Kevin 7
Pawełczyńska, Anna 34
Petrov, Vladimir 65
Philippines 10, 13–14, 15, 49, 99
Pinter, Harold 110
Piteşti (Romania) 70, 89

Pohl, Oswald 1
Poincaré, Raymond 20
Poland 43, 111, 112
Potsdam Agreement (1945) 83
POWs 6, 11, 20–1, 24, 27, 37, 39, 43, 63–4, 103

R

Rajoy, Mariano 110
Rauschning, Hermann 31
Ravensbrück 40, 52
Reale, Luigi 72, 73
refugee camps 3, 23, 71, 94–5, 104, 112
Resnais, Alain 34
Rhodesia 87
Rigoulot, Pierre 88
Risiera di San Sabba (Italy) 73
Roberts, Stephen H. 31
Rodrigo, Javier 75–6, 108
Roma ('Gypsies') 4, 40, 44, 72
Romania 88–9
Roosevelt, Franklin D. 77
Rosenfeld, Isaac 36, 106–7
Rossi, Jacques 58
Rousset, David 34, 51, 70–1
Russia 6, 23, 27
Russian Revolution (1917) 23, 27, 52

S

Sachsenhausen 32, 37, 38, 40, 43, 76, 83
San Nicola (Italy) 72
Schmitt, Carl 96
Schnell, Felix 51, 63
Schulze, Rainer 109
Schwarze Korps, Das 32
Semprun, Jorge 52–3
Sevpechlag (Soviet Union) 57
Shalamov, Varlam 56, 57
Shifrin, Avraham 64
slavery 10
Slovenia 73

Smith, Iain 11, 16
Sobibór 4, 40
Sobol, Joshua 110
Sofsky, Wolfgang 34
Sokolov, Andrei 54
Solovetski Islands 53, 54
Solzhenitsyn, Alexander 51, 55, 57, 65
Somalia 73
South Africa 2, 10, 11, 13, 14–17, 15*f*, 16, 24, 27, 32, 34, 49, 96, 99, 105
South Korea 95
Soviet Union *see* Gulag
Sovnarkom 54
Spain 2, 6, 48, 75–6, 110
    Civil War 24, 37, 70, 75–6
'special settlements' (Gulag) 2, 50
Sri Lanka 93
Stalin, Joseph 55, 59, 64, 65, 84, 103, 110
'state of exception' 3, 7, 24, 96–8, 105
St Cyprien (France) 74
Stucki, Andreas 11
Stutthof 39, 40
Suderland, Maja 34
Suny, Ronald 26
Sweden 93
Syria 94, 114
Szajna, Józef 110

T

Taft, Elise Hagobian 25–6
Takayoshi, Ichiro 97–8
Tanganyika 85
Tasmania 10, 12
    see also Australia
Theresienstadt 21
'Third Reich'
    see Nazi Germany
Times, The 23
Todorov, Tzvetan 34, 51–2, 53
Togo 22

Tomasinlag (Soviet Union) 57
Transnistria 44, 69
Treblinka 4, 26, 40, 64
Trnopolje (Bosnia) 92
Tunisia 71
Tuol Sleng (Cambodia) 90
Ţurcanu, Eugen 89

U

Uganda 85
Ukhtpechlag (Soviet Union) 55–6
Ukraine 44, 83
United Nations (UN) 112
United States of America 2, 11–12,
    13–14, 63, 69, 70, 81, 95–6,
    97, 106
  Air Force 89
  Army 109
  DP Act (1950) 81
  Indian Removal Act (1830) 11–12
  internment of Germans 79
  see also Japanese-Americans,
    detention of
UN Refugee Convention (1951) 22
UNRRA 82

V

Van Heyningen, Elizabeth 15,
    16*b*, 17
Ventotene (Italy) 72
Vietnam 87, 90
Vietnam War 89
Voigt, F. A. 31

Völkischer Beobachter 32
von Estorff, Ludwig 18
von Falkenhausen, Alexander 28
von Trotha, Lothar 28, 29
Vorkuta (Soviet Union) 55, 56, 57,
    58–9, 60
Vorkutlag (Soviet Union) 56
Vyshinski, Andrey 68

W

Wachsmann, Nikolaus 39, 97
Ward Price, George 31–2
Werth, Nicolas 57, 67
Weyler, Valeriano 13
Wikipedia 92–3
Williams, Philip 90–1
Winton, Nicholas 112
Wu, Harry 91
Wu, Yenna 90–1
Wyschogrod, Edith 34

Y

Yale University 89
Yarl's Wood (UK) 98
Yodok (North Korea) 92
Yugoslav Wars 2, 92

Z

Zeilsheim (DP camp) 81
Zhong Ma 27
Zionism 81
Zwart, Joop 40–1

Index

SOCIAL MEDIA
Very Short Introduction

Join our community

www.oup.com/vsi

- Join us online at the official Very Short Introductions **Facebook** page.
- Access the thoughts and musings of our authors with our online **blog**.
- Sign up for our monthly **e-newsletter** to receive information on all new titles publishing that month.
- Browse the full range of Very Short Introductions online.
- Read **extracts** from the Introductions for free.
- If you are a teacher or lecturer you can order inspection copies quickly and simply via our website.

HUMAN RIGHTS
A Very Short Introduction
Andrew Clapham

An appeal to human rights in the face of injustice can be a heartfelt and morally justified demand for some, while for others it remains merely an empty slogan. Taking an international perspective and focusing on highly topical issues such as torture, arbitrary detention, privacy, health and discrimination, this *Very Short Introduction* will help readers to understand for themselves the controversies and complexities behind this vitally relevant issue. Looking at the philosophical justification for rights, the historical origins of human rights and how they are formed in law, Andrew Clapham explains what our human rights actually are, what they might be, and where the human rights movement is heading.

www.oup.com/vsi

NUCLEAR WEAPONS
A Very Short Introduction
Joseph M. Siracusa

In this *Very Short Introduction*, the history and politics of the bomb are explained: from the technology of nuclear weapons, to the revolutionary implications of the H-bomb, and the politics of nuclear deterrence. The issues are set against a backdrop of the changing international landscape, from the early days of development, through the Cold War, to the present-day controversy of George W. Bush's National Missile Defence, and the threat and role of nuclear weapons in the so-called Age of Terror. Joseph M. Siracusa provides a comprehensive, accessible, and at times chilling overview of the most deadly weapon ever invented.

www.oup.com/vsi